Mommy's
RAINY DAY
SURVIVAL GUIDE!

Linda L. McKnight

At-Play Publishing

Dedicated to my son Brayton,
may we never suffer another boring rainy day!

Disclaimer

This book is designed to provide information in regard to the subject matter covered. The purpose of this book is to educate and entertain. This book should not be considered a substitute for the advice of competent professionals in the fields of child development, child physiology or the advice of your family physician.

All children are unique. Parents and teachers know their own children and students best. Therefore parents and teachers should evaluate their children's and student's tendencies prior to conducting the activity suggestions in this book. Parents and teachers are ultimately responsible for the appropriate care and supervision of their children and students.

The author and At-Play Publishing shall have neither liability nor responsibility to any person or entity with respect to any loss or damage caused, or alleged to be caused, directly or indirectly by the information contained in the book.

If you do not wish to be bound by the above, you may return this book to the publisher for a full refund.

Contents

Section I

1. Introduction 7

2. What to Do When They're Climbing the Walls!!!

3. They Still Have Energy Left to Burn. Now What???

Section II

1. Art & Other Creative Ideas

2. Dramatic Play Ideas

3. Kitchen Kreations

4. Measuring, Sifting, Sorting & Stringing

5. Painting Ideas

6. Science Ideas

7. Sensory Activities

8. Table Top Activities

Introduction

It's been raining cats and dogs for days! The coming week's weather forecast doesn't look good, more rain is on its way. As the wind howls outside and the rain beats against your windows, you helplessly watched your precious little angels transform from the children you know and love into uncontrollable—*monsters!* Cabin-fever has set in bad! They are behaving like wild animals. Your children are tired of being cooped up, they're bored, and literally climbing the walls. You are tearing your hair out. You have had it with the rain and with your children acting like maniacs. What to do? How can you tame the rainy day beast within your children without imposing marshall law? It's time to resort to survival skills. *"Mommy's Rainy Day Survival Guide"* to the rescue!

This book comes to you from the trenches, a preschool classroom!!! I am a former pre-school teacher of 14 years. Rainy days were always the pits! I dreaded them! They were exhausting! Imagine contending with not just one, two or maybe three children, but ten to twelve (or more) rambunctious children all at one time. That's twelve sets of legs all going in different directions, all at the same time. Yikes! It's even frightening to us preschool teachers who are seasoned professionals. Rainy days are, more often than not, a challenge for all who care for young children—period!

Although I loved working with preschoolers, rainy days were the exception. I enjoy working with children much more when they are under control, pleasant and manageable, which they are much more likely to be when they have ample opportunity to burn off excess energy by running around outside.

Why I wrote this book.

I wrote this book for the simple reason that I could not find *IT* anywhere else. Necessity being the mother of invention—you know. Surprisingly, there are not many rainy day activity books available. As difficult a situation as rainy days can create, it has always puzzled me that there were not several dozen on the market to choose from.

So, because of my occupation (which was responsible for my dislike of rainy days), I was always on the lookout for a great rainy day book. Despite my exhaustive search, I never found a book that, I felt, had the right collection of activities to be my lifesaver on a rainy day. Sure, there are hundreds of children's activity books with thousands of wonderful activity ideas in them but, most of the activities in other "general" activity books required too much advanced planning to be of much help on a rainy day.

On a rainy day you need great ideas *right now!*

In my experience as a preschool teacher, on a rainy day you need not just ideas, but *great* ideas to keep active children busy *right now!* You also need an array of activities that really hold children's interest. You have all of that energy to contend with and all of that outside time to make up for and not much, if any, time to plan. I wanted a rainy day book that was a treasure-trove of activities that I could literally open to any page, at any time of the day, and have a simple, yet terrific, I already have all the materials, no planning necessary, activity idea right there waiting for me to put it into action. As simple as this idea sounds, until now there was not such a book available (at least I never found it).

But that's not all, I also wanted, yet never found, a children's rainy day activity book that also included activity ideas specifically designed to *constructively* burn up all of that boundless energy children develop when they are cooped up. As anyone who has ever cared for young children quickly learns, children who are filled to the brim with wild energy cannot calm themselves down just because you *tell* them to.

Furthermore, it is unreasonable to expect young children, who are naturally energetic, to manage themselves calmly for extended periods of time on a day when they cannot go outside to run off steam. So, if they cannot go outside to run around, naturally they are going to run around inside, *it's only natural!*

This creates quite a dilemma. Children *need* to run, jump, spin, climb, bounce and so on and so on but, children running amuck in the house can drive most adults crazy. They are not being rambunctious *just* to drive you crazy (really they're not). Their little bodies are just *full* of energy. What children need on rainy days are practical ways to work off excess energy—*inside*. Sounds logical doesn't it?

Children need a way to BURN off excess energy!

The simplest solution to out-of-control energy is to find *controlled* active activities to occupy children—inside—in place of outside time. Children need a way to work out that energy. In other words, *burn* it off. But *what* do you do? *How* can you help children burn off all of that excess energy? Do you find that you can't think of anything under pressure? Do *you* find (as I always did), yourself suffering from brain-freeze? Creatively paralyzed! Unable to think of a single interesting thing for your children to do in an emergency like this?

Do you find the only thing that keeps racing through your mind is how you wish the sun would come out, NOW, so that you could send your children outside to run around and blow off steam? Do you wish your children would simply calm themselves down, but find that they simply just can't. Do you desperately wish you had an idea for a magical (messless) activity that would keep your children busy and happy for the next couple of hours so that you could regroup, regain your sanity and maybe even get *something* done?

Join the crowd, every adult who has ever cared for young children (since the beginning of time) has had those very same feelings! In fact, there is a saying in the child care industry that goes something like this "A teacher is not fully appreciated until the Monday following a rainy weekend." Isn't that the truth! That is precisely why I wrote this book. To rescue anyone who cares for young children (Moms and preschool teachers alike) from the terrible fate of unruly youngsters on a rainy day. Thankfully, there is plenty you can do *inside* to bring children back down to earth but, without the right resource at your fingertips, you're doomed!

How this book came to life.

Since I couldn't find what I was looking for written by someone else, I always thought that someday I might write my own rainy day activity book (if for nothing else to rescue me from my own children on rainy days). But like most people who have an idea for a book, I never had the time. Being a preschool teacher keeps one pretty busy and at the end of the day there just isn't much energy left over for weighty projects like writing a book, I'm sure you can imagine.

Well, in 1994 I became pregnant with my first child and decided not to return to work. I wanted to be a stay-at-home Mom. After my son was a few months old, I began looking around for idea books for babies (my education was mainly for preschoolers 2yrs–6yrs). I had no idea how to entertain a baby.

I assumed I could just run down to my local library and find several good books on the subject. Wrong! Lots of books *about* babies, but few about what to *do* with your baby for entertainment. I even went to my neighborhood teacher's supply store and special ordered a couple of infant activity books. I was rather disappointed with what I received. This situation just spurred on my quest even more.

About this time a little voice in my head started making noises about writing "my own" activity book. As I looked for activity books for my son, I eventually became convinced that writing my own activity book wasn't such a bad idea. After giving it some serious thought, I decided to pursue the rainy day angle since that had always been such an issue for me.

Furthermore, I suspected that if rainy days were such a frustration for me with the benefit of years of training and "in the trenches" experience dealing with it, then undoubtably, it must also be a difficult ordeal for Moms at home with their children. I began researching and found that the idea I had for putting together the "right" kind of rainy day activities had not been done the way I wanted it done and decided to "go for it."

I started with ideas for activities that could be used at the drop of the hat.

I started by collecting a list of miscellaneous simple activities that could be used at the drop of a hat. The kind of activities where most people already have all the ingredients and/or materials around the house or schoolroom. I then worked to collect indoor activities that anyone could use to help children burn off excess energy.

Next, I searched through years of my collected curriculum ideas looking for more involved activities that fit into "my" criteria of great rainy day activities. What I came up with is an arsenal of super duper, never fail, tried and true, *save me now God*, activities that are simple to set up and only require ordinary supplies that most people already have on hand and/or can easily get a hold of at a local grocery or hardware store. I even include a complete list of all the ingredients and/or supplies you will need to conduct any of the activities. You will find this list on page 154. The list was designed to be easily photocopied and kept in your wallet so that it is handy every time you go to the grocery store, hardware store, or craft store.

What makes the activities in this book so special?

While gathering my list, I had very specific types of activities in mind. I looked for simple, yet lengthy, (time consuming) activities that had "staying power." Activities that children generally really, really enjoy and can become very involved in and play with for an extended period of time (hopefully to give Mom or teacher some peace). After all, after going to the trouble to set up an activity for your children, you at least want it to last for a while. Lengthy activities also encourage damage control (the mess factor). If your children are involved in the same activity for a good length of time, then you don't find yourself spending all of your time cleaning up mess after mess. There is only one mess to clean up. Yeah! What a concept!

The activities in this book have no end.

In my quest I also searched for open-ended activities. Most of the activities in this book are child-directed and have "no end." In other words, activities in which children will not "complete the project" then need something else to do. My goal was to put together a group of activities that would allow children to play with, create with, and enjoy until *they* were finished. I also wanted plenty of activity ideas that would provide an array of opportunities for "discovery" and "imagination-building."

Besides, projects and activities that "make a product" generally are activities in which *someone else* used their imagination to create the idea, then children just "do." Children get a lot more from open-ended activities that encourage them to use their own imagination and creativity rather than *making something* that someone else thought of first. I believe children learn most effectively by making their own discoveries.

Additionally, another problem with "make something" types of activities is that soon after starting the project your children "finish" the project and then they have to find a new project or something else to do. On a rainy day, you need activities with substance. Activities that will continue to keep children busy *without* having to go from project to project because they keep reaching a prescribed "end," leaving you with bored, restless children all over again. This may not be as much of an issue on the home front, but in a preschool setting you need to keep children engaged or you face possible mutiny. Nothing can turn on you faster than a group of preschoolers with nothing to do—they can whirl out of control in the blink of an eye.

You are holding in your hands the result of my search for great activities.

So the adventure began, I gathered my list, and what you are holding in your hands is the result of my search for fabulous, simple, open-ended, lengthy, minimal mess, rainy day ideas and activities that really hold preschoolers interest. The ideas and activities in this book will entertain and amuse your children, as well as burn off abundant wild energy, in a way that will delight them and bring <u>you</u> back into control. In my opinion, it is *THE* activity book to have for young children on a rainy day or any day. It is a fantastic resource for anyone who cares for young children and especially Moms at home with their wonderfully rambunctious children. So here it is, a book of terrific rainy day, keep'um busy and off the walls activity book.

All the activities in this book have been kid tested, mother and preschool teacher approved for fun and safety. Many of the activities are old standbys in child care centers all around the country, however many are originals from my own kitchen. I truly hope you find *Mommy's Rainy Day Survival Guide* a valuable, or better yet, *invaluable* tool for getting through those long rainy days.

What to do when...
your children are:

CLIMBING THE WALLS!!!

Your children are in orbit . . .

They are climbing the walls and driving you crazy! They seem to have five times more energy on a rainy day than on a non-rainy day. It's true, children do have lots and lots of energy on rainy days. They have all of that excess energy leftover from not running around outside. *Calgon take me away!!!* It's time to fight fire with fire! **What better way to zap that energy than to "burn it off."**

In this first section I will be giving you ideas of ways to "exercise" your children so that they can work off all that excess energy in a way that is tolerable to you. The idea here is to channel or redirect their energy into something that is acceptable with you. If your children are running around the house and you tell them to stop running, what happens? They run faster and jump higher! Yikes!

Change your strategy! Instead of telling them to stop running—stop them from running randomly. Take control of the situation. Give them an agenda so that they can work off their energy in a constructive way. For example, _Tell_ your children to run up and down the hall five times (or more). After they have run up and down the hall a few times they will be able to sit down for a few minutes and do a puzzle or something quiet. They may amaze you and tell you after a couple of times up and down the hall that they are tired and want to sit down. Hallelujah!

On to the activity ideas. . .

Balloon Volleyball: This is one of my favorites. Balloon volleyball really gives children a good workout. This will work best if you have two or more children. Just blow up a few balloons (round ones) and let your children bat them back and forth together. You might need to push your furniture out of the way so that no one runs into the coffee table, but that's all there is to it. Children have a really good time with this activity and it is terrific for syphoning off excess energy.

✂ **_Supplies You Will Need_** ✂
- ☆ Large, round balloons. Please use caution; balloons are a choking hazard for small children!
- ☆ Lots of open space.

☺ **_Ways to Expand this Activity_** ☺
- ☆ Confetti in the balloons will make rattling sounds when they are tossed around.
- ☆ You can set up a "basketball hoop" and let your children try to shoot hoops.
- ☆ You can give your children each a straw and have them blow the balloons around the house, maybe even give them an obstacle course to follow.
- ☆ You can draw all sorts of different things on the balloons (faces, shapes, letters, numbers etc.) to make things a little more interesting. Ask your children what they would like drawn on their balloon.
- ☆ **_Balloon Tennis:_** Now, just when things are starting to simmer down and your children are beginning to loose interest in the balloons, give them tennis rackets. No, not real tennis rackets, homemade tennis rackets made out of empty cardboard paper towel rolls and paper plates (stapled and taped together). If you don't have any paper towel rolls available you can use a section of a cardboard box or a rolled up newspaper. Now you have a whole new game. Let your children bat the balloons around with their rackets.

Basketball: Cut out a hoop shape from a good size piece of cardboard and hang it up in a place where there are no breakables (taped to a door, stuck into a kitchen cabinet etc.). A nerf ball is the ideal "basketball," but lots of things will work, bean bags, rubber balls, a small stuffed animal, even a wadded up piece of paper or aluminum foil will work.

✄ *Supplies You Will Need* ✄
- ☆ 12 x 12 or so piece of cardboard.
- ☆ A "basketball."

☺ *Ways to Expand this Activity* ☺
- ☆ Use a wastebasket as the "hoop."
- ☆ Make a game out of who can throw it the farthest; increase the distance with each throw.

To make your own bean bags, for temporary use, fill a few socks with beans, rice or even noodles then tie the top of the sock in a knot.
Simple Dimple!!!

Bowling: Children love to knock things down. Here is a way for your children to really get in some good "knocking things down" time. Your children will be in heaven! Furthermore, bowling is a game that just about any child (at any age) can have fun with. All you need are a few plastic bottles to use as "pins" and any kind of ball. For "pins" you can use plastic (1 liter) soda bottles, ketchup bottles, hairspray bottles, shampoo and/or conditioner bottles, empty milk cartons etc. You can stand the bottles upright the way they normally stand or if your children are a little older and need more of a challenge, you can stand them upside down on the neck of the bottles.

For a bowling "ball" you can use Koosh balls, bean bags, *any* ball and/or a real bowling ball. Even a wadded up piece of aluminum foil or newspaper thrown at the "pins" will do the job.

✂ _Supplies You Will Need_ ✂

- ☆ Bowling pins.
- ☆ A bowling ball.

☺ _Ways to Expand this Activity_ ☺

- ☆ After your children begin to lose interest in the standard bowling methods try using other things as "pins." For example, empty video tape container produce the domino effect when they are knocked down. Some old books or wooden blocks are another thing that produce the domino effect when knocked over. Even duplo blocks stacked together will work as "pins." You have a lot of options available.

- ☆ Now, when you have exhausted your resources for new "pins", have your children try to NOT knock down the "pins." In other words set up an obstacle course so-to-speak and see if your children can roll a ball through the "pins" *without* knocking them down. This will present quite a challenge.

Dancing: Let your children dance to the radio. If you want to jazz things up a bit let them dance with scarves in front of a mirror. The scarves are to make it more interesting and your children will stay with it longer. The mirror is, again, to make it more interesting, but it is also for self-esteem building. Children love to look at themselves in the mirror and this way they can look at themselves "doing something." Children often become engrossed looking at themselves in the mirror, so this is a good activity to just stand back and watch what happens. Maybe take a video, it will be great fun to watch in a few years.

✂ ***Supplies You Will Need*** ✂

☆ Scarves, scraps of material, an old tie of Dad's or whatever else you can find.

☆ Open space.

☆ A full length mirror. If you don't already have one you can buy them at the hardware store for about $10 and they store away very easily.

☺ ***Ways to Expand this Activity*** ☺

☆ Break out your old disco records or other dancing music you have hidden away. How fun! The library also has lots of dancing type music available. They also have dancing music for kids that can be checked out.

☆ Play dress up first, then dance (this would make an exceptional video for the archives).

☆ If you know how to dance yourself maybe you can teach your children how to dance (line dancing, polka, square dancing, the macarena, the hustle, etc.).

Exercise with a video or TV exercise show: If you have cable you know there are a hundred different "exercise shows" on all the time. Use them to your advantage. Even if you are not interested in exercising yourself, let your children follow along.

✂ _Supplies You Will Need_ ✂

☆ TV or an exercise video. Find a program that is for beginners or low impact.

☺ _Ways to Expand this Activity_ ☺

☆ Exercise video for children. There are several exercise videos for children on the market (believe it or not). Mattel® has a children's exercise video called Barbie's Total Workout Tape available at Blockbuster Video and at Toys R Us.

Flashlight Tag: You will need to darken a room for this activity. It is not necessary to have total darkness but the darker the room, the better the effect. Give everyone a flashlight. Cover one of the flashlight lenses with colored cellophane to make the light from that flashlight colored. The colored flashlight is "it." The rest of the group is supposed to "get" the colored light. Loads of fun!

✂ _Supplies You Will Need_ ✂

☆ Flashlights and colored cellophane. Just plain flashlights are fun for children too.

☺ _Ways to Expand this Activity_ ☺

☆ Draw shapes, letters, numbers, teddy bears etc. on the cellophane before covering the flashlight lens.

☆ If you don't have any cellophane, use plastic wrap and color it with a permanent felt marker.

☆ You can also cover the end of the flashlight with a piece of aluminum foil and cut a shape out of the middle of the aluminum foil to set it apart from the other flashlights.

☆ This is a good birthday party game.

Hide-and-Go-Seek: You probably already play this with your children, nevertheless I wanted to include it anyway, just in case. Nothing gets the old adrenaline flowing in children more than a good old fashion game of Hide-and-Go-Seek. For the purpose of using up excess energy, I would suggest playing Hide-and-Go-Seek until your children call it quits.

✂ ***Supplies You Will Need*** ✂
    ☆ No supplies needed.
☺ ***Ways to Expand this Activity*** ☺
    ☆ Take turns being the hider and seeker, that will stretch the game out longer.
    ☆ Instead of just counting numbers while the hiders hide sing a song or recite the alphabet.

Children love repetition! If they want to do the same activity over and over, "go with it."
You may get tired of the repetition but children learn from repetition. If
they're happy and learning, you're way ahead of the game!

Jumping off the Couch: **This may sound like a crazy idea but, it really will bring your children back down to earth if they are full of energy and driving you crazy. You might first want to cover your couch with a blanket to protect it. Then, just let your children loose. They will have a ball.**

This activity will also help your children develop depth perception. They will learn by jumping from the couch to the floor "how far away they are from the floor." This is how children learn depth perception, by jumping off of something onto the floor. You may have already had battles with your children trying to get them to *stop* doing this, but unbeknown to you, they were doing it for developmental reasons.

✄ *Supplies You Will Need* ✄

☆ **A couch or even a bed.**

☺ *Ways to Expand this Activity* ☺

☆ **Have your children jump from the couch into a hula hoop or onto a towel laid out on the floor. Give them a target, something to aim at. See who can jump the farthest!**

☆ **If you have a mini trampoline, let them jump from the couch to the trampoline and back.**

A MOMMY TIP

One thing that we found worked quite well at the school was to have the children do really physical things in the morning, to work off all that energy, then they would be able to take a good nap. After naptime we would do lower key activities like painting, cooking, playdough, dress-up etc. Then before you know it, the day is over and we could declare victory over another rainy day!!!

Jumping on the Bed: I know, I know, *WHAT!!!* Yes, you read correctly, jumping on the bed. Now, I realize that every child in America has been told to *STOP* jumping on the bed. If you think about it though, they really are not going to hurt the mattress. If a 100+lb. adult spends at least eight hours every night tossing and turning on that mattress, then a child who weighs 30 or 40 lbs. jumping for 10 or 15 minutes is not going to put excess wear on the mattress. Besides, the benefits are great! Your children will work off their excess energy and have a *BLAST* doing it. Of course, use discretion, and, needless to say, this is a supervised activity.

There are many other benefits as well. Jumping, in general, stimulates the vestibular system in the inner ear. This stimulation in turn develops balance and helps develop areas in the brain that your children will need to develop before they learn how to read. Jumping is *GREAT* for children! Let them go for it!

Now, if you are concerned about them falling off and injuring themselves (which of course is a possibility), then just take a few precautions. Cover the nightstands with pillows and have a "rules" talk beforehand. If you are concerned about "what if they jump when I'm not looking." I would just explain to them that it is OK to jump on the bed, but only when they ask first, and you are available to supervise.

My son has always been allowed to jump on the bed and he has never wanted to jump by himself. He always wants me to hold his hands and "jump" with him. Yet of course, you know your own children best! If this activity seems like it may create a problem in the future, just don't ever start allowing your children to jump on the bed in the first place.

✂ *Supplies You Will Need* ✂
☆ Just yours or your children's bed.

☺ *Ways to Expand this Activity* ☺
☆ Sing "Five Little Monkeys Jumping on the Bed."

Five Little Monkeys Jumping on the Bed...

Five little monkeys jumping on the bed.
One fell off and bumped his head.
Mama called the doctor and the doctor said "No more monkeys jumping on the bed!"

Four little monkeys jumping on the bed.
One fell off and bumped his head.
Mama called the doctor and the doctor said "No more monkeys jumping on the bed!"

Three little monkeys jumping on the bed.
One fell off and bumped his head.
Mama called the doctor and the doctor said "No more monkeys jumping on the bed!"

Two little monkeys jumping on the bed.
One fell off and bumped his head.
Mama called the doctor and the doctor said "No more monkeys jumping on the bed!"

One little monkey jumping on the bed.
One fell off and bumped his head.
Mama called the doctor and the doctor said "No more monkeys jumping on the bed!"

Jumping on a Mini Trampoline: This is an alternative to jumping on the bed. If you have one of those exercise trampolines, they are great for children too. They are a real lifesaver on a rainy day! Children get the same workout on one of those as they do running around the house. The great benefit is that they stay in one place so they don't drive you crazy. We literally wore out several trampolines over the years at the preschool. _They are worth their weight in gold when you have rambunctious children around._

✄ _**Supplies You Will Need**_ ✄

☆ A mini trampoline. (They are often available for about $10 at garage sales and flea markets).

☺ _**Ways to Expand this Activity**_ ☺

☆ Count jumps, sing the ABC's to the jumps, or give your children a scarf to wave around. If you give your children a scarf and put them in front of a full length mirror, you may never get them off. They will absolutely love it!

A MOMMY TIP

Have you read the introduction to this book? Take a moment and skim through it. You will gain insight as to my motivations for writing this book and the specific reasons why I chose the activities I did. Reading the introduction may also give _you_ insight, allowing you to consistently be one step ahead of your children (on a rainy day) when you need to be.

Log rolls, somersaults, wheelbarrow walks and spinning: None of these exercises really need an explanation, but here are some great ideas for using up energy!

Log rolls - Have your children log roll back and forth across the family room floor. Have a race. See who can get from one side of the room to the other the fastest. See if your children can count their rolls while they are rolling. This seems simple but, it can be tricky to do both.

Wheelbarrow walk - Wheelbarrow walk your children all over the house. Wheelbarrow walking stimulates the inner ear. This stimulation has a calming effect. If you wheelbarrow walk your children to bed, for naps and bedtime, they may be able to fall asleep more easily.

Somersaults - Have your children somersault their way to breakfast, lunch etc. Then, maybe a few "laps" of somersaults up and down the hallway whenever they start to get restless. Personal note—My son loves doing this. It really works on getting him to calm down! This is also a neat trick you can use to get your children to be willing to go off to bed, somersault their way! Your children will be in bed and fast asleep before you know it.

Spinning - Doesn't this one drive you crazy? Most children go through a "spinning" phase; all they want to do is spin around the room all the time, and again, they are doing it for developmental reasons. You can use this to your advantage. Have your children spin until they are spun out. Give them a scarf or two to hold while spinning. Pretty soon they will be good and winded and ready for a break, then you get one too. Give them a puzzle or a book, pour yourself a cup of coffee and enjoy the calm!

Make an Obstacle Course: How fun this can be. The possibilities are endless. Give your children a route to follow. Have them walk around the kitchen table 3 times. Then, go into the living room and crawl under the coffee table (which is covered with a blanket for effect). Next, go do a somersault on the bed etc. See if they can remember everything you told them to do and maybe play follow the leader if necessary. If your children are old enough to follow a map, try giving them a map. Then, after they have had fun with your map, see if they can make up their own route and their own route map to follow.

✂ _Supplies You Will Need_ ✂

☆ The supplies you will need will depend on what you have available in your house.

☺ _Ways to Expand this Activity_ ☺

☆ You can have your children run the obstacle course in all sorts of different ways: fast, slow, very slow, backwards, doing somersaults, crawling, etc. <u>A few words on crawling</u>, if your child(ren) did not crawl very much before they began to walk, then it is important that they spend some time crawling before they begin to learn to read. This is a very involved subject. This book is not intended to cover those aspects of child development, however crawling is very important for developing the parts of the brain that we use to read. Children who didn't crawl enough may have problems learning to read. If your children did not crawl much, I suggest you discuss it with your pediatrician to get more information. There is also an excellent book available called "Sensory Motor Integration" by Jean Ares which explains, at length, how important crawling is. The good news is that if your children didn't crawl much when they were babies, you can help them make up for it by intentionally giving them crawling activities now (even after they are well past crawling age). Whenever you think of it have your children crawl around the house, on the way to the bathroom, on the way to lunch etcetera, they will just think you are being silly; little do they know. . .

Riding Tricycles: If you have a garage or carport and your children have tricycles or bicycles, let your children ride around out in the garage (providing it isn't too cold outside).

✄ _Supplies You Will Need_ ✄
    ☆ Bicycles, tricycles and/or Little Tykes wheel toys.
    ☆ A covered area.

☺ _Ways to Expand this Activity_ ☺
    ☆ You can make a course for them to ride through by drawing "roads" on the floor with chalk.

Roller-skating: Another garage activity.

✄ _Supplies You Will Need_ ✄
    ☆ Roller-skates. Keep your eye out for roller-skates at flea markets and at garage sales. You will see them often and can buy them very reasonably.

☺ _Ways to Expand this Activity_ ☺
    ☆ Skate to music, just like at the rink.

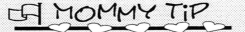

A MOMMY TIP

Important parenting tip. Remember to "catch" your children being good!
Several times daily ☺ !

Ring Around the Rosy: **To use up more energy and hold their interest longer than the standard way of playing *Ring Around the Rosy*, have your children "spin" rather than hold hands and turn around in a circle. With arms extended (and maybe a scarf or two), teach them the words to *Ring Around the Rosy* (if they don't already know them).**

♪ ♫ **"Ring around the rosy,** ♪ ♫

♪ ♫ **A pocket full of posies,** ♫ ♪

♫ ♪ **Ashes, ashes,** ♪ ♫♪ ♪ ♫

♪ ♫ **We all fall down."** ♫ ♪ ♫

✄ ***Supplies You Will Need*** ✄

☆ **Just a few scarves for your children to wave around while spinning and singing.**

☺ ***Ways to Expand this Activity*** ☺

☆ **I thought this would be a good place to list a few other ideas for carpet games.**

Charades (Of course, this is for children who are a little older)
Duck, Duck, Goose
Hiding and Finding (One child hides something, the other finds it)
Hopscotch (Make a hopscotch pattern, made out of tape, on a blanket)
London Bridges
Mother May I
Red Light, Green Light

Houston, we have a problem!

OK! So, They're Not Thundering Through the House Anymore!

It's time for a little break in the action. By now your children are no longer running around like crazy people, but they are still pretty energetic. You are tired and ready for things to calm down. Therefore, we need some in-between activities that still put all that energy to use, but with less exuberance. In this next section, the ideas are less rambunctious yet providing equal entertainment value.

The following group of ideas will use up their extra energy and not totally drain yours. Many of the following activities were carefully selected because they are activities that you can get your children started on and then they should be able to play on their own and entertain themselves. This will produce busy, happy children and a break for Mom! Hallelujah!

The ideas in this section will have your children building with boxes, crawling, chasing paper airplanes and making forts. All the things children love to do but can't seem to think of when they are bored. *Mommy's Rainy Day Survival Guide* to the rescue!

Build a Town: You will need a roll of butcher paper for this activity. Costco sells rolls of nice thick butcher paper that would be perfect for this activity. Roll out several lengths of butcher paper and tape them together (side by side). Then, draw roads, trees and houses etc. on the paper. Have your children build buildings for the town out of Legos, Lincoln Logs or blocks. This should keep them busy for quite a while. They can also wheel their cars and trucks around on the roads.

They do make a pre-made town on material that you can buy at the fabric store, but making the town yourself is half the fun. There is also a "town" carpet available at Home Depot and at various children's stores, but I think it is too small. I have also noticed that children tend to get bored with always having the same pattern. By making your own you can add things as needed or change things and it is a family project rather than something you bought at the store.

✂ _Supplies You Will Need_ ✂

- ☆ Butcher paper or an old sheet that you don't mind donating to your children, even a few paper grocery bags taped together will work just fine.
- ☆ A big black felt pen for drawing roads, trees and buildings.
- ☆ Legos, Duplos, Lincoln Logs, blocks or anything else to make buildings out of.
- ☆ Your children's cars, trucks and little figurines (to be townspeople).

☺ _Ways to Expand this Activity_ ☺

- ☆ Use a nice big piece of heavy fabric and you may have a goldmine of free time on a rainy day. If you make your town out of sturdy fabric you can roll it up and save it for the next rainy day. Then, you can build on what you already have. Your children will love it even more the second time around because they already know what to do and they can build on their previous experience.

Building Forts: **Remember this from when you were a child? Forts, cubbyholes and castles make wonderful fun for children. They love having a special hideaway to play in.**

✄ *Supplies You Will Need* ✄

☆ **Blankets or sheets.**

☆ **Something to make into a fort, kitchen table, coffee table, bunk bed, etc.**

Fortress Ideas . . .

Appliance boxes are one of the best forts. They are just the right size for children. They are portable, very versatile and they are also "new" so-to-speak. You know how children always love "new" things? But where do you get an appliance box without buying a major appliance? You have to keep your eyes open for this one. Call around and see if someone will save you one, you might strike gold. In my area there is a large appliance retailer who is more than happy to share their large cardboard boxes. Whenever we needed one for a school activity, they were happy to oblige. If your children would really get a bang out of a cardboard fort, it may be worth it to call around to a few appliance retailers.

Drape a blanket over the top bunk of a bunk bed and make the bottom bunk "the fort."

PVC Pipe can be used to make a fort (also see pg. 40). PVC pipe is very reasonably priced and you can do just about anything with it. It is very, very versatile. Use your imagination, I bet you can come up with several great designs. Then, cover with a blanket or sheet.

Use PVC pipe to make a tepee. Six or eight lengths of PVC held together by a belt or rope and covered by a sheet, blanket or a few towels will do just great. Your children will be in "fort" heaven!

Pitch a tent. If you have a small (no stakes in the ground) backpacking tent, there you have it, the ultimate fort. You may not see your children for a week! They will probably want to eat all their meals, take their naps and go to bed in the tent. You could really expand on this idea too. Take hikes, go on bear hunts, have picnics, eat s'mores, you know, follow the whole camping theme. What fantastic memories you will be helping your children to build!

A MOMMY TIP

Children are process, not product, orientated. In other words, most of the time they are not "making" anything, they are just doing. For example, when a three year old builds with blocks he/she is just building for the pleasure of knocking it down when they finish. Children generally do not have an agenda, it's *getting there* that is all the fun! At the preschool we did not ask the children "what" they were making we asked them to tell us "about" their project.

Building with Boxes: This is another winner! Start saving all of the boxes that food comes in. Tape the box tops closed and when you have collected a dozen or so let your children build with them. Your children will especially like to knock them down. When the boxes wear out, toss them and replace with the next empty box to come out of the kitchen.

✂ **_Supplies You Will Need_** ✂
- ☆ Empty food boxes (cereal, crackers, pot pie, juice cans, egg cartons, etc.).

☺ **_Ways to Expand this Activity_** ☺
- ☆ Children also like to play "kitchen" with empty food boxes.
- ☆ Give your children a roll of masking tape and let them tape the boxes together. If they are a little older and more skilled, they might be able to make a "target" in the boxes to throw a nerf ball or paper airplanes through.
- ☆ After your children are done building and are ready to do something else, let them paint their box sculpture. Pizza, cereal, cracker and cookie boxes plus paper towel, toilet paper and wrapping paper tubes all make very interesting and fun sculptures when glued or taped together. Then the fun just keeps on going when they get to paint it.

Catch: Make scoops out of plastic milk cartons and play catch with a ball.

✂ **_Supplies You Will Need_** ✂
- ☆ Plastic milk or juice cartons with handles (well washed).
- ☆ A nerf ball if you have one, but any ball will do or even a rolled up ball of aluminum foil or newspaper wadded up and taped into a ball.

☺ **_Ways to Expand this Activity_** ☺
- ☆ Take this out to the garage or covered patio, if it's not too cold.
- ☆ Instead of using milk cartons as "catchers" use plastic Tupperware type bowls to catch with.

Fishing Game: Here is an all-time favorite. Let your children mosey on down to the pond for some fishin'. All you need to do is straighten out some wire coat hangers, attach some string or yarn and attach a magnet to the end of the string. If you don't have any magnets handy, you can use the magnets on your refrigerator as "bait." To make "fish," cut out "fish" shapes from paper, attach a paper clip and let the catching begin.

✄ _Supplies You Will Need_ ✄

- ☆ Fishin' poles, you can use coat hangers, wooden dowels or even a piece of newspaper rolled up tightly, taped at the ends, then attach string for a line.
- ☆ Magnets.
- ☆ Fake fish.

☺ _Ways to Expand this Activity_ ☺

- ☆ To make this even more fun, let your children fish in a plastic wading pool (without water). Your children will get a fantastic kick out of if. Oh what fun! What wonderful cherished memories you will be helping your children to build!
- ☆ You really don't even have to make "fish." You can just use regular playing cards, 3 x 5 cards (with fish drawn on them), flash cards, etc. Whatever you find around your house that you can attach a paper clip to will be fine. Your children won't be particular. They will just enjoy the challenge of trying to "catch" the target with the fishing pole.
- ☆ Juice can lids make really good fish too. The magnetic area is big so they are easy to pick up.
- ☆ If you do make a homemade fishing game, be sure and save the pieces. Your children will be thrilled the next time you bring it out for them to play with.
- ☆ There are several commercially made fishing games available in your local toy store. Since this is such a popular activity with young children, I might suggest purchasing one and stashing it in your "Mommy's Rainy Day Survival box."

Follow The Leader: Do your children complain when one follows the other one around the house? Probably, most children get irritated when their brother or sister copies/follows them. This time make it a game! Have big brother follow little sister through the house (under the kitchen table, around the coffee table 2 times, out to the garage, etc.). Now, when they start to get bored with this, switch places and have little sister follow big brother for a while.

Next, when this gets old, try suggesting somersaulting down the hall, making funny faces at each other or copying each other's clapping hands or stomping feet pattern. If one or both of your children are creative and/or clever and a bit on the "ham" side, this activity just might help keep them busy, happy and entertained for a while. Plus, you all might get a couple of good laughs out of what they come up with.

✂ _Supplies You Will Need_ ✂

☆ Just your children's imagination's!

☺ _Ways to Expand this Activity_ ☺

☆ I think the possibilities are endless. As long as they don't get on each other's nerves, your children could play follow the leader/copy each other for hours.

⌂ MOMMY TiP

You've heard the expression "Busy Hands Are Happy Hands"? Well, I couldn't agree more. I am a firm believer that boredom breeds discipline problems! Keep your children _constructively_ busy and you will have fewer discipline problems.

Paper Airplanes: At first, this may not seem like a very physical activity but, when you think of all the running back and forth your children will be doing to retrieving their airplanes, you realize that this very well could work off quite a bit of energy. Children love paper airplanes. I have made *thousands* of them as a teacher. You don't need to be the least bit fancy about it either, as long as it flies your children will be happy. The trick is to teach your children how to fold their own planes so that you can go do something else while they are busy with this activity.

✄ ***Supplies You Will Need*** ✄

☆ Paper to fold into airplanes. Save flyers that come in the mail and you will have all the paper airplanes your children could ask for.

☺ ***Ways to Expand this Activity*** ☺

☆ You can have contests to see who can make their plane fly farthest (make sure everyone gets a turn to win).

☆ You can have your children aim at a target or try to fly their plane through a hoop. You can use the same hoop you used for the basketball activity on page 18.

☆ Your children may want to color on their airplane and/or add streamers.

☆ Your local library will have books on how to make fancy paper airplanes. And, there is yet another thing you can do on a rainy day, plan to go to the library just for paper airplane books.

PVC Pipe and Marbles: This is an absolute guaranteed winner! It's cheap; no set up is required; very little supervision is necessary; your children will love it, and it will keep them busy for quite a while. Best of all, it is a very clean activity, there is not much of a mess to contend with.

Visit your local hardware store (this could be part of your rainy day activity). Buy 5 to 10, 10ft. lengths of PVC pipes with matching connectors and a hacksaw if you don't already have one. When you get home cut the PVC pipe up into smaller lengths about one, two and maybe even three feet long. If you don't feel you can cut the PVC pipe yourself, ask the sales clerk in the plumbing dept. of your hardware store to cut the pipe for you. My local Home Depot will cut PVC pipe free of charge into whatever lengths wanted, you just have to ask.

That's all there is to it. Give your children the short pieces of PVC pipe, connectors, and a few marbles. Now, you get to sit back and watch what happens. Your children will build and connect the pipes together, roll the marbles through, then build and connect some more and may find hours of just plain fun. This activity is one of my personal favorites. I feel it is a terrific activity because it really challenges children's minds by offering almost endless possibilities for assembling different sized and shaped structures. Furthermore, there is no right or wrong way to build, it is up to your children's imagination!

✄ _Supplies You Will Need_ ✄

- ☆ PVC pipe and connectors. Be sure to sand/file off any sharp edges. Five 10ft. lengths of PVC pipe and 60 connectors cost me about $15.00 at Home Depot.
- ☆ Marbles.

☺ _Ways to Expand this Activity_ ☺

- ☆ If you have very small children and are concerned about marbles and choking, you can buy larger PVC pipe and use plastic golf balls or ping pong balls (ping pong balls are smaller, so if you use them, the size of the PVC pipe would be also smaller, saving you money).

Sidewalk Chalk: Sidewalk chalk is a popular activity! But, on a rainy day, all the sidewalks outside are wet. Head for the garage. The garage floor will do just fine as a surface to draw on, providing it's not too cold. You can either let your children draw at will and/or you can use the chalk to make something specific like the hopscotch pattern or shapes. Then, let your children play hopscotch or jump from shape to shape.

✄ **_Supplies You Will Need_** ✄
  ☆ Chalk.

☺ **_Ways to Expand this Activity_** ☺
  ☆ If you want to make the chalk designs semi-permanent, dip the chalk into Vano® starch before drawing with it and the designs will stay visible longer. You may want to do this if you are drawing a hopscotch pattern or road that you are going to want to use again in a few days.

Simon Says: I'm sure you remember how to play Simon Says from your own childhood, but just as a reminder here is how you play: Give your children an action of some kind (touch your toes) but say "Simon says touch your toes," "Simon says touch your head" etc. Your children have to listen carefully as to whether you say "Simon says" first or not. If you *do* say "Simon says" first then your children are to follow the direction given. If you *do not* say "Simon says" first then they are to ignore the direction and wait for the next one. Whoever moves after being given a direction in which "Simon says" is not said first, is out of the game.

✄ **_Supplies You Will Need_** ✄
  ☆ None

☺ **_Ways to Expand this Activity_** ☺
  ☆ Use your children's names in place of "Simon." This is **great** for self-esteem!
  ☆ This might help at clean-up time. "Simon Says" pick up all the *red* blocks, *blue* blocks etc.

Splish Splash: Take a bath! If your children are _really_ full of energy and need to shift from wild to calm, a bath just might do the trick—even if they're already clean!

✂ _Supplies You Will Need_ ✂

☆ Just a bathtub full of water.

☺ _Ways to Expand this Activity_ ☺

☆ Add some different toys to the bath water like measuring cups from the kitchen and/or other kitchen utensils, baby dolls, toy trucks, etc.

☆ You might kill two birds with one stone by getting your children's toys clean at the same time.

☆ Would your children enjoy listening to their favorite sing-a-long tape while they bathe?

☆ Blowing bubbles is another way to extend the bath time activity. Give your children a container of bubble solution and a wand (saved from a store bought bottle of bubbles). You can make your own bubble solution with a 1/2 cup of Dawn® dishwashing liquid and 1/4-1/2 cup of water and 1-3 teaspoons of glycerine (optional-glycerine is available at the drug store).

☆ Another way to blow bubbles in the bathtub is to give your children a couple of straws and let them blow air into the water and make bubbles. <u>Make sure they know not to _drink_ the water.</u>

☆ Another neat thing to add to the bathtub is clean paintbrushes. Your children may like the feeling of "getting painted."

☆ <u>Special hair washing trick</u> — Do your children <u>HATE</u> to have their hair washed because the water and soap runs down their face? A solution to this problem is to tape something to the ceiling above the bathtub for your children to look at (I made a happy face on a paper plate for my son). When you are wetting and rinsing their hair, tell them to look up at the happy face. While looking up at the ceiling, their heads will be tipped far enough back that the water and soap will all run off the back of their heads and not down onto their face. ☺

Straws & Ping Pong Balls: Let your children have a ping pong ball race across the family room floor. Not much explanation need here. Give each of your children a straw and a ping pong ball, see who can get the ping pong ball across the room first.

✄ _Supplies You Will Need_ ✄
- ☆ Straws.
- ☆ Ping pong balls or you can make light-weight balls out of aluminum foil.

☺ _Ways to Expand this Activity_ ☺
- ☆ Have the race on a table or set up come kind of course or maze to weave the ping pong balls through.

⌨ MOMMY TiP

Warning! Warning! It's time to clean up!

Clean up time will go a lot smoother if you give your children 5 to 10 minutes of advanced "warning" that it's almost time to do something else. Children often have a hard time with transitions, a few minutes forewarning gives them time to mentally prepare for a change of activity. A timer is a great way to give your children a little "power" in the decision making. Ask _them_ how long to set the timer for, give them a choice of three, five or ten minutes. When the timer goes off it's time to clean up.

Treasure Hunt: Have your children go on a treasure hunt. FUN! First, have your children hide their eyes, then hide things around your house and give your children clues as to where to find them (you know, warmer/colder).

✄ *Supplies You Will Need* ✄

☆ Something to hide, you can hide everyday things from around the house or go for *real* treasure (a new toy, candy or maybe something fun like a new bottle of bubbles).

☺ *Ways to Expand this Activity* ☺

☆ Try drawing a "hidden treasure" map for your children to follow and find the "treasure."

☆ Use one of your children's puzzles to play treasure hunt with. Hide the pieces of the puzzle around the house. Then, as your children find the pieces, have them reassemble the puzzle.

☆ You can also make a matching game from paper and tagboard or cardboard. Cut 10 or 12 circles out of a piece of paper. Trace the same number of circles onto a piece of cardboard or large piece of paper. Number both, the circles on the cardboard, and the corresponding cutout circles. Now, hide the cutout paper circles around the room and as your children find them match them up to the traced circles on the cardboard. This may be a way to begin to teach your children about numbers, letters, shapes and colors. You can really be creative with this activity. Use different colors of paper, different shapes, even fabrics and after a while your children will be able to play this by themselves. I used to use this idea to make games on special holidays at the preschool. For instance, for Valentine's Day I would cut out 12 hearts from red paper and trace the same number of hearts onto a piece of poster board. I would hide the paper hearts around the classroom and have my preschool students look for the hidden hearts. The children really liked this activity. We would play it over and over. I did the same thing for the rest of the holidays (shamrocks for St. Patrick's Day, eggs or bunnies for Easter and so on throughout the year).

Woodworking: At most cabinet shops or construction sights you can get scraps of wood that your children can pound on, glue on and paint on. This is another real favorite. Of course, at first you will want to be on hand for close supervision and to teach your children how to handle a hammer. Pretty soon they will be old pros. This is a good activity that Dad can get in on over those rainy weekends.

✂ _Supplies You Will Need_ ✂

- ☆ Wood scraps.
- ☆ Nails.
- ☆ Hammers and other tools. Children love to work with real tools.
- ☆ Glue (instead of nails if you prefer) and things _to_ glue, bottle tops, gallon milk container tops, baby food jar lids, scraps of fabric, etc.

☺ _Ways to Expand this Activity_ ☺

- ☆ When your children are finished hammering and/or gluing let them paint their work of art or color on it with felt markers. This is a project that they will be very proud of.

**PHEW!!! We have achieved splashdown!!!**
**Your miniature astronauts have reached the earth. Thank Heavens!!!**

Start a Priceless Collection

Have you ever noticed that, quite often, children have several different "sets" of connect together type toys (Legos, tinker toys, duplo blocks), yet none of the "sets" work together nor are they big enough to really build something terrific with? <u>BORING!</u>

What if. . . you started a "collection" for your children? Each birthday and gift-giving holiday is an opportunity to add to the collection. Before long you will have a pretty expansive "set" of manipulative type toys for your children to build and create with. Imagine what a 5,6 or 7 year old can do with a lego set that has a couple thousand or more pieces. Wow! They could really get involved with a set like that!

When choosing what you want to start "collecting," consider something that will grow with your child. Legos, for example, are great because very young children can use them well, then as the children grow they can continue to get a lot of use from them. As children's attention spans grow so does the complexity of their projects. Legos can be used for very simple building when children are young and very elaborate projects as children grow and become able to build more complicated structures.

Here's an added bonus, after years of accumulating a good size set of toys, you will have something of considerable value. Once your children have outgrown the collection it might be sold for a tidy sum. There is big money in used children's toys. Or the collection could be kept on hand for when other young children visit and/or handed down to the grandchildren.

Yikes! Can you imagine—GRANDCHILDREN!

Now for some quieter activities . . .

Now we're getting into old familiar territory. . .

Here is where we get into the old familiar as far as activities for young children go, "Arts and Crafts." The difference here is that I have chosen this particular group of activities due to their "staying power," with respect to attention span. What I mean is, these activities are all the very favorites. They all tend to hold children's attention for a decent length of time as opposed to the five minute crayon and paper activity.

After years of trying hundreds of art projects and craft ideas, the list that follows is the best of the best, most popular activities that nearly every child will love to do over and over again, even if you have 120 straight days of rain or snow.

Collage: This is an old standby activity. You will probably remember this one from kindergarten yourself. Have your children glue or paste things onto paper. Good old Elmer's glue works best. They can glue just about anything, scraps of paper, cutouts from magazines, styrofoam packing peanuts, ribbon, yarn, buttons etc. and/or whatever else you can find around your house.

✂ _Supplies You Will Need_ ✂

- ☆ Scraps! At the preschool each teacher had a "scraps" box filled with all sorts of things suitable for collage. When the box got full enough (which never takes very long), then it was collage day. You can do the same thing at home and pretty soon you will have a good collection of collage "stuff" too.
- ☆ Paper for gluing onto.
- ☆ Glue. Little bottles of Elmer's glue make fun stocking stuffers.

☺ _Ways to Expand this Activity_ ☺

- ☆ If you want to make this an academic activity you can write letters/numbers/shapes on the paper and let your children glue packing peanuts to the letters/numbers/shapes.
- ☆ Glue popped popcorn, dried beans, elbow macaroni noodles, leaves, scraps of fabric etc.

MOMMY TiP

Save flyers that come in your mail for your children to draw, color and paint on the back.

Karo Syrup and Food Coloring: This activity has a very neat end result. Pour a small amount of Karo syrup on a paper plate. Have your children gently tip the plate in circles to spread the syrup around. When the Karo syrup is thinned out a bit add a few drops of food coloring. The drops of food coloring should be spaced a couple of inches away from each other. That way, as your children tip and turn the plate, the colors will mix together and create new colors.

After your children have tipped and mixed the syrup and food coloring, set the paper plates aside to dry. If the weather is very humid it could take up to a couple of days to dry completely. When finished, the paper plate will be very colorful and *very* shiny. It really looks neat! One thing to be careful of is not to get too much syrup on the plate. If the plate becomes too wet it will take a very long time to dry.

✄ Supplies You Will Need ✄
☆ Paper plates. For best results—use <u>paper</u> plates not styrofoam.
☆ Karo syrup (liquid corn syrup).
☆ Food coloring.

☺ Ways to Expand this Activity ☺
☆ After the Karo syrup is dry, you can cut the edge off of the paper plate and hang it up in a window.
☆ These make beautiful window decorations!
☆ Let your children blow the food coloring around in the Karo syrup with a short straw.
☆ Let your children mix up the syrup and food coloring with Q-tips or toothpicks.

Life-size Silhouettes: **This is a neat experience for children. Have your children lay down on the floor on top of a piece of butcher paper. Draw an outline of their body on the paper. Now, let them "decorate" themselves. You can get really elaborate with this and use yarn for hair, buttons for eyes and real material for clothes. Or you can just let your children color on the paper.**

✄ *Supplies You Will Need* ✄
- ☆ **Large butcher paper.**
- ☆ **A big black felt pen to draw the outlines of your children's bodies.**
- ☆ **Crayons, watercolor felt pens, regular watercolor paints or tempra paint.**

☺ *Ways to Expand this Activity* ☺
- ☆ **If you wanted to make their life-size drawing three dimensional, cut out two outlines of their bodies, staple the front and back together (leaving an opening), then stuff with newspaper.**
- ☆ **Let your children cut out their own silhouettes.**

⌨ MOMMY TiP

If your children tend to wander off while you are shopping and/or they are just getting to the age when they don't want to ride in the stroller anymore. Try giving them a bell to wear around their neck or tied to their shoelaces. I "let" my son wear my "Christmas Bell" when we are shopping. He thinks it's cool to wear the bell. But the big picture, for me, is peace of mind. Even if he steps around a corner I can still hear him "jingling." I always know where he is every second!

Melted Crayon Art: This is a neat activity but, it requires a great deal of supervision. You will need an electric skillet or griddle (a griddle works best) set on its lowest setting. Place a piece of aluminum foil on the griddle and hold it in place with wooden clothespins (plastic ones might melt). Next, have your children draw on the foil with crayons. The crayons melt as they touch the heat and create a neat effect on the foil. Have a couple of hot pan holders handy for your children to rest their empty hand on. Otherwise, they may just put their other hand right on the griddle. I have seen many near misses. Please be very careful! If fact I would suggest having a talk about rules before you begin. An ounce of prevention you know!

✄ **_Supplies You Will Need_** ✄
- ☆ An electric skillet or griddle. USE CAUTION! USE CAUTION!*
- ☆ A set of crayons with half of the paper removed.
- ☆ Sheets of aluminum foil about the same size as the surface of the appliance.

☺ **_Ways to Expand this Activity_** ☺
- ☆ Instead of foil you can use other things to draw on like regular white paper, construction paper, paper plates or even sturdy paper towels. Very fine grit sandpaper will work too and then you have a sort of "sandpainting effect." You can also use fabric to draw on, but you need to use a fabric that is on the stiff side. Wallpaper from sample books will work well too.

  * **Never allow your children to come near the heated griddle when you are unavailable. Turn the griddle off and move it out of reach if you need to tend to something else. Also, try to set yourself up with the electrical cord out of the way so that no one trips over it.**

Object Rubbings: "Object" means just about anything flat. Coins, leaves, keys, puzzle pieces, the cutouts left over from the paper plate stencils you made (see pg. 146), paper folded in funny shapes, etc. Using a regular piece of paper, place an "object" underneath it and use the flat side of a crayon to "rub" over the object. The object will leave an impression on the top side of the paper.

✂ **_Supplies You Will Need_** ✂
   ☆ Anything flat, finding objects to rub is half the fun.
   ☆ Paper.
   ☆ Crayons with the paper removed.

☺ **_Ways to Expand this Activity_** ☺
   ☆ Cut the "rubbing" out of the paper.
   ☆ For special holiday days you can rub appropriate shapes and have your children make "Happy Holiday" signs. For example, rub heart shapes with red and pink crayons then write "Happy Valentines Day" on top of the paper. Rub shamrock shapes with light and dark green crayons for St. Patrick's Day and so on, you get the idea. Then, maybe your children can use the "signs" as place mats for lunch and dinner on that day.
   ☆ You could also make "Happy Birthday" signs on larger pieces of paper and hang the paper in your kitchen on birthdays of your family members. The rubbings could be of candles and balloons cut out from other pieces of paper.
   ☆ Rubbings on larger pieces of butcher paper can also be used as special wrapping paper for birthday and holiday presents.

Puffy Hanging Art: Here is a display alternative to the refrigerator door. By now it may have been years since you have seen the front of your refrigerator, no doubt it has been covered with precious works of art. Instead of trying to find room for another work of art, hang it. Any piece of artwork, which is on paper, can be made into a hanging piece of artwork. All you do is cut out another piece of paper the same shape as the original artwork. Staple the two pieces of paper together (leaving an opening), stuff newspaper between the two pieces of paper, then finish stapling. After you have made your artwork "puffy," attach string/yarn to the top and hang it from the ceiling or in window (hang it from the curtain rod).

Your children will especially appreciate the extra recognition that their "hanging" art will attract. It also makes for a festive look around special days (hearts for Valentine's Day, four leaf clovers for St. Patrick's Day, pumpkins for Halloween, etc.).

✂ _Supplies You Will Need_ ✂

☆ Paper cut to the same (roughly) shape/size as artwork.

☆ Stapler.

☆ String or yarn.

☆ Newspaper for stuffing.

☺ _Ways to Expand this Activity_ ☺

☆ Your children can decorate both sides of the hanging art.

☆ Decorate with paint (tempra or watercolor), felt pens, scraps of paper, fabric, sequins, pictures cut from magazines etc.

☆ If your children are a little older, you can try having them "sew" the pieces of paper together with yarn instead of stapling and/or let your children staple the paper together themselves.

Tissue Paper & Liquid Starch: This is a really easy activity, it's easy to set up and clean up. All you will need is paper to "paste" on, tissue paper and liquid starch. Cut the tissue paper into small shapes (squares, circles, triangles, hearts, letters, number etc.). Then, let your children "paste" the tissue paper shapes onto paper with the liquid starch. The starch acts as a glue and is transparent, so you can see the different layers of tissue paper underneath the top layer.

✀ *Supplies You Will Need* ✀

- ☆ Paper, most any kind of paper will do.
- ☆ Tissue paper cut into shapes. You can use tissue paper used for wrapping presents if you have a couple of different colors or you can buy tissue paper in the craft store. Usually you can buy a variety package so that you will have a rainbow of colors to choose from.
- ☆ Liquid Vano® Starch.
- ☆ Paintbrushes.

☺ *Ways to Expand this Activity* ☺

- ☆ The tissue paper and liquid starch is a very versatile project. Your children can decorate bottles (if you don't want them working with glass, plastic bottles will well work too). The bottles can become vases or tin cans to hold pencils or anything else you can think of.
- ☆ You can add glitter or confetti to the starch and as your children are painting on the starch they will also be adding glitter/confetti to their project.
- ☆ This activity can be used with appropriate colors and shapes to celebrate a holiday. You can cut out red, white and pink hearts for Valentines Day or green four leaf clovers for St. Patrick's Day and so on throughout the year.

Tie-dye: This is simulated tie-dye (although real tie-dyeing is an idea for a rainy day activity, I think it is pretty messy and too involved for small children). For this activity your children will be making designs on coffee filters with food coloring.

Coffee filters are just the right absorbency for this activity. When your children drop drops of food coloring onto them, the food coloring spreads out very nicely into pretty designs. When two different colors run together, they blend into the respective new color. Children really seem to like this activity and it is a terrific way to teach them their colors.

Start by mixing some food coloring with a small amount of water. Let your children use eye droppers to drop the water onto the coffee filters. Be prepared to go through a lot of coffee filters. Children really like this activity.

✄ _Supplies You Will Need_ ✄

☆ Coffee filters, you need the kind that lay flat when spread out. Any size will do.

☆ Food coloring of all the primary colors (red, blue and yellow).

☆ Eye droppers.

☺ _Ways to Expand this Activity_ ☺

☆ Instead of food coloring use watercolor paints.

☆ This will work on paper towels too, but coffee filters look prettier in the end.

☆ You can also cut the coffee filters into different shapes and/or into snowflakes both before your children tie-dye them and after they are done.

☆ After the coffee filters are dry, make flowers out of them by gathering them up in the center and tieing them off with a pipe cleaner.

☆ These also look neat hanging in a window.

The Wonderful World of Ivory Snow: Ivory Snow is an amazing thing. You can do loads of things with it besides laundry. Here are some fun things you can do with it.

Bathtub Crayons - Wouldn't your children have a blast drawing pictures on the bathtub wall? Of course they would! Here's how to make bathtub crayons at home.

Mix together - 1 c. Ivory Soap Flakes
¼ c. Warm water
Several drops of food coloring

Whip together in a blender until smooth. Pour into muffin tins or any other mold you have around that will make small chunks for your children to draw with. After the soap has dried, pop them out of their molds and let the creativity begin.

Floaty Soaps - This is similar but just a bit different. Make floating soaps for your children's bath time. You know that Ivory Bar Soap floats in the tub? Well soap made of Ivory Soap Flakes floats too, and you can make soap into any shape you want at home. Here's how you do it.

Mix together - 1 c. Ivory Soap Flakes
½ c. Boiling water
Several drops of food coloring (optional).
Scent - Perfume or food flavorings work great and add a lot of fun to the soaps.

Again, whip everything together in a blender. Next, pour the mixture into cookie cutters to give the soap interesting shapes. Let dry. Presto, fun soaps for bath time. Don't worry about your walls, Ivory Soap bathtub crayons and floaty soaps will wash off the bathtub walls.

Wax Paper Wonder: This is another old standby that you may remember from your own childhood days. Start by having your children collect leaves. They can be somewhat dried out and if it is in the fall then the different fall colors will really add to the outcome of this project.

After you have collected an assortment of leaves, you and your children will need to make some very small crayons pieces. You can do this two ways. You can do this using a cheese grater and "shave" crayons into tiny pieces. But, then the cheese grater probably won't be safe for grating cheese anymore (your neighborhood thrift shop may have an old cheese grater for sale). Or you can break up a few crayons by putting them, one at a time, into plastic sandwich bags and giving them a few good whacks with a hammer. They will break up into small pieces and you can break them up even more with your hands.

Now, after all your preparations are complete, you can begin assembly. Take two sheets of wax paper and arrange your leaves and crayon shavings on one of the sheets. Place the other sheet on top of the one with all of the decorations on it.

Next, "press" the two sheets of wax paper together with a warm iron (the iron should be on the very lowest setting). As the crayon melts in-between the sheets of wax paper it produces a beautiful effect. Your children will be so very proud of their beautiful artwork!

Sometimes crayon gets onto the iron while doing this. I suggest putting a couple of sheets of newspaper on top of the top sheet of wax paper and press through the newspaper. When you and your children are finished, let the iron heat up to the hottest settings and wipe it with clean paper towels. This will prevent any crayon from getting onto your clothes the next time you use your iron.

✂ *Supplies You Will Need* ✂

☆ An assortment of leaves in different shapes, sizes, colors and even different states of decay.

☆ Crayon shavings.

☆ Wax paper.

☆ A warm iron.

☺ *Ways to Expand this Activity* ☺

☆ You can add all kinds of things to the inside of the wax paper, glitter and/or sparkly confetti, cut out letters and/or numbers, or cut out words from magazines.

☆ You can make a frame from construction paper and frame the wax paper art.

☆ Make the wax paper into different shapes (a heart, a circle, a triangle), then put a frame around it.

☆ You might arrange cut up pieces of colored tissue paper in-between the wax paper.

ᕦ MOMMY TiP

When you have accumulated several crayon bits, you can make *new* multi-colored crayons by putting a few small handfuls into muffin tins. Put them in your oven at 250 degrees until the crayons begin to melt into each other. You will need to keep an eye on how fast they are melting. If the crayons melt too much then they will just turn yukki black (that's no fun). After they are melted just set them out to cool and you will have new crayons.

Un-Birthday Present Gift Ideas . . .

Coming up with new and interesting things to give your children as presents can be difficult some times. The following is a list of gift ideas that are out of the ordinary and are guaranteed not to be thrown in the closet never to be used, worn or played with. Fun! Fun! Fun!

Briefcase filled with paper, felt pens, scissors, crayons, colored pencils, stencils, watercolor paints, tape, glue stick, stickers, stamps and a stamp pad, and envelopes.

Cereal, the trashy brand that your children love but you hate and won't normally buy. Let them eat it for dessert, after a good solid meal, rather than for breakfast.

First-aid Kit, Hours of fun!

Metal box or fishing tackle box with padlock and key.

Small suitcase with overnight bag for toiletries including sample size soap and shampoo.

Photo album with pictures of your children, family and maybe a special friend.

Broken appliance for the "curious and always taking things apart child." Include a small set of screwdrivers. Be sure to cut off any cords. Visit your local thrift shop.

Dress-up kit, choose an idea from the Dramatic Play section and collect the parts.

Wigs and hats, children love wigs and hats. Visit your local thrift shop.

Give your children the "gift of time"! Give a coupon booklet with coupons redeemable for one-on-one time with Mommy or Daddy: 30-minutes of time playing in their room. A trip to the movies with "just" Mommy. A trip to the park. A bike ride around the block with "just" Daddy. The gift of time!

Cabin-Fever Productions

presents....

RAINY DAY THEATER

Children love to play "dress-up," that's a given. Why not make it just a little more interesting? Give them a theme. Here are some ideas to start with. I'm sure you will be able to expand the list. Oh yes, remember to load your camera with film and charge up your video camera battery!!!

Any of the ideas listed here would make terrific dress-up "kits" to be given as a gift. I build my dress-up kits at the thrift shop instead of the toy store. I have given dress-up "kits" to children for birthday presents and always hear rave reviews from the parents weeks after the child's birthday. Children always get a lot more out of gifts that encourage them to use their imagination as opposed to a "toy" that can only be played with one way.

Although there are several ideas listed below, there are a few "essential" pieces of equipment needed that your children can use for any dress-up theme.

1. First, a nonworking real phone for your children to play with. Children love real phones!
2. Next, your children will need play money. Play money can be made on scrap paper. Play money is also a great stocking stuffer or birthday gift.
3. Paper in different sizes, loose and in note pads along with pencils and felt pens.
4. Stamps and a stamp pad. Children can stamp travel tickets, receipts, mail, etc.
5. Stickers. Children can find a million uses for stickers, even during dress-up.

Airplane: Choose who is to be the pilot, flight attendants and passengers and "dress up" accordingly. Choose your destination and what you will be doing there, remember your luggage. Have a pleasant trip!!!
Kit ideas: Luggage (with destination tag) dress sport jacket for boys, fancy hat and jacket for girls, maps, airline tickets, captain's hat, pilot's wings, magazines for reading while in flight, airline type plates with "compartments" to serve lunch in.

Carpenter: Let your children pound nails into wood scraps. With a little practice they will get pretty good at it. At the hardware store they have tools that are small enough for children to use and children really love wood working. Styrofoam sheets (not packing peanuts but solid styrofoam sheets) make good "wood" if you don't have any real wood scraps around. Styrofoam sheets are available at most hardware stores. Golf tees can substitute for nails when using styrofoam. Balsa Wood is also great for this activity. Balsa wood (hobby shops sell it) is very soft and easy to drive nails into.
Kit ideas: Real hammer, real nails, wood scraps, real hand-held drill, toy saw, tape measure, ruler, tool belt, hard hat, pencil, clipboard, paint and paintbrushes.

Store: Give your children various items that a clerk in a supermarket would use. A cash register, apron, play money, coupons, paper pads, pencils/crayons, paper bags and empty food boxes. Make play money on scraps of paper.

Office: Give your children "office" supplies. Paper, pencils or crayons, children's scissors, tape, envelopes, stamps and a stamp pad, a hole punch, return address labels, stickers etc. Of course they will need a "real" nonworking phone. Thrift stores are great places to buy real phones as play toys. Children love real phones!

Princess & Prince: Here is an all-time favorite! Children LOVE pretending to be royalty. I guess it's only natural, who doesn't like to be waited on hand and foot and to give everyone else orders? With the right equipment your children could be in "Royal Heaven." You can really build on this theme by picking out books from the library that are about Kings, Queens and their royal subjects (Snow White, Cinderella and Robin Hood). <u>Kit ideas:</u> The next time you are at the thrift shop remember to look for Royal looking things (very shiny jewelry, clothes with sequins or gold thread, veils, very dressy shoes, ethnic costumes from different countries, etc.). You can make crowns and scepters from aluminum foil.

Train: You will need a conductor, an engineer and passengers. Have your children make up special tickets for special destinations. Maybe your children would like to eat their lunch in the diner car? Let their imaginations do the rest. <u>Kit ideas:</u> Luggage, maps, train tickets, conductor's hat.

Theater: Your children may get a real charge out of this one. Go all out, let your children get dressed up really fancy. Maybe even paint their fingernails (boys like this too but, if *you* don't like that idea you can use clear polish or water). To extend this idea you could rent a special video and really "watch" something.

Here are a few additional ideas that your children may enjoy beyond the ideas listed above: Wedding, Post Office, Beauty Parlor, Doctor's Office, Firefighter, Police Officer. If your children are "dramatically inclined" you may suggest they act out a story. In other words, "act out" Little Red Riding Hood or The Three Bears or put on their own play. Don't forget your video camera!

KITCHEN KREATIONS

What Better Way to Tame Your Children than with Food?

You probably have several cookbooks around your house already. But I felt that this wouldn't be a well-rounded activity book if I didn't include some old-time favorite children's recipes and cooking projects.

What I went for in this section were unusual cooking projects. I have included recipes that are mostly nutritious but, some are just for fun. I made a point to stay away from sugary recipes because that is the last thing you need on a rainy day. Most of these recipes have something for your children to "do" rather than recipes that require you to do all the work and your children to just "watch." Bon Appetite!

Tip about sweets . . . What we found to work really well at the preschool was to not serve the children sweets until the afternoon. All of our birthday parties were held in the afternoon (after naptime) so that the children weren't all wired up on sugar before their nap.

Alphabet Food: Here are several neat, simple ways to make food into alphabet letters.

Alphabet Biscuits: Using the pre-made Pillsberry crescent roll biscuits dough, unroll all the crescent roll dough and cut the dough into strips. Shape the dough strips into the letters of your children's names or use alphabet letter cookie cutters to cut letters out of the dough. Children get an extra charge out of eating their name.

If your children are too young to understand what alphabet letters are, let them cut "shapes" out of the dough with cookie cutters. They can eat "star" biscuits or "gingerbread man" biscuits. Cook the biscuits in a toaster oven or electric skillet so that your children can *SEE* the dough puff up, rise and turn golden brown.

Alphabet Cookies: This time use pre-made sugar cookie dough. Cut the letters of your children's names out (or shapes). Then, let your children decorate the sugar cookie dough with sprinkles or paint (milk, food coloring and new watercolor paintbrushes). Another option would be to wait until the cookies come out of the oven and let your children frost their cookie letters with pre-made frosting, cream cheese (with food coloring in it), peanut butter, etc.

Alphabet Soup: At most grocery stores you can buy alphabet noodles in the pasta section. Make your own homemade alphabet soup with a can of chicken broth and a handful of alphabet noodles. Of course, you can add just about anything else to the soup to jazz it up a bit, carrots, celery, corn, peas or anything else your children can think of.

Serve your alphabet soup with your alphabet biscuits and discuss the letters of your children's names and maybe the letters of your name and other people's names that your children know. What a fabulous way to begin to learn about the alphabet!

Applesauce: Applesauce is a nutritious and easy to prepare snack that most children like. They will especially _love_ it coming from their own kitchen. There are several different ways to make applesauce. With peels or without, chunky or smooth, with cinnamon or without, with sugar or without--it's really up to you. We have made applesauce every way possible at the preschool and it comes out fine every time. You will need about one apple per child and it really doesn't matter what kind of apple you use. If you do plan to use a tart apple, plan to add some sugar or maple syrup.

Getting started: Wash, dry, peel (optional) and core your apples. If your children are old enough to handle a butter knife, let them cut the apple up into chunks. If you don't feel comfortable giving your children knives, you might slice the apples into thin slices. Then, have your children cut the apples into small pieces with cookie cutters, a pizza cutting wheel, or a pastry blender. The apple pieces do not in any way, shape, or form need to be in uniform chunks. If you want a smooth applesauce, small chunks are not necessary, just put big chunks into the blender and puree.

Next, you are going to cook the apples. If you have an electric frying pan this would be a good time to use it so that your children can see what is going on and you won't have to have them standing on chairs over the stove (use extra, extra caution regarding the electrical cord).

Saute the apples (chunks or puree) over medium heat for 15 or 20 minutes until tender. If you have a Teflon pan then you really don't need to add any oil. If you don't I would suggest a teaspoon or so of cooking oil or margarine (butter burns) to make sure the apples don't stick and burn. Let your children stir while the apples are cooking. Stirring gives them something to do.

As the apples are cooking, add whatever "extra" you want (for example: sugar, cinnamon, raisins, walnuts and maybe a little butter right at the end to add flavor). Ask your children for suggestions, they may come up with something really terrific. Yet, even if they get silly and suggest something like chocolate chips or marshmallows, as long as it is relatively reasonable, I would "go with it."

After all, you are not necessarily making applesauce for nutritional value. You are making applesauce with your children to broaden their horizons and give them good healthy (emotional) childhood memories to look back on. Most importantly though, making applesauce will provide relief from suffering boredom on a long rainy day.

✂ *Supplies You Will Need* ✂

☆ Apples. Whenever possible use organic apples. Apples are one of the most heavily sprayed crops (this goes for organic apple juice too).

☆ An electric fry pan (optional).

☆ Blender.

☆ Condiments: cinnamon, raisins, nuts, etc.

☆ Cutting utensils - butter knives, pizza cutters, cookie cutters etc.

☺ *Ways to Expand this Activity* ☺

☆ Add other flavors of fruits: cherries, peaches, apricots, blueberries, strawberries, raspberries.

☆ If you want to get really different you could add almond or peppermint flavoring.

☆ Add food coloring for an added kick!

Coffee Can Bread: This is a very interesting project. Any bread recipe that you have can be baked in a metal vegetable/soup/fruit/coffee can. This is a project that I did as a child in Elementary School and I have very fond memories of it. I thought it was so neat to have my own personal loaf of bread. I have always remembered it. I plan to do this often with my own children. Your children will also have fond memories of _Coffee Can Bread._ There is just something special about home baked bread. Then, to add to the specialness of it, if your children each have their own personal loaf, that "they don't have to share with anybody if they don't want to," you have something extra special!

Start by washing out metal cans. If you run them through the dishwasher, remove them promptly and thoroughly dry them or they will rust. After you have collected a few cans, then you can make _any_ bread recipe. Instead of putting the batter into a loaf pan, put it into the metal cans (they need to be well greased). Fill the cans one half to three quarters full and place the cans on your oven rack positioned in the center of your oven. Use the temperature recommended in the directions but the time allowed for baking will be different. You will have to monitor your bread. Check often to make sure that your bread doesn't become over done.

Once your breads are done, allow them to cool laying on their sides. After 15 or 20 minutes see if they will slide out of the cans. If not, slide a knife down in-between the side of the can and the bread. Work your way around the can until the bread comes loose. If all else fails, cut the bottom of the can off and push the bread out. Now, everybody has their own bread! Your children will be tickled!

✂ *Supplies You Will Need* ✂
☆ Metal cans.
☆ Bread dough.

☺ *Ways to Expand this Activity* ☺
☆ If you don't want to go to the trouble to "make" bread. Use pre-made dough available in the freezer section at your grocery store.

☆ Make pull-apart cinnamon bread. Using any yeast bread recipe, prior to the last rise, roll your dough into doughnut hole size balls. Glaze each ball with melted butter and roll in cinnamon sugar. Arrange the dough balls gently in your tin can, let rise for 20-30 mins then bake. Your house will be filled with the aroma of fresh baked cinnamon bread. What a special treat!

☆ I recently saw a gingerbread cake that had been baked in a vegetable can at a specialty grocery store. If "bread" is too much trouble (letting it rise and all), bake a cake in vegetable cans or coffee cans instead.

☆ Make banana bread, coffee cake, poppy seed cake in coffee or vegetable cans.

☆ This activity would make a fun holiday gift to give to neighbors, teachers etc.

☆ You can also use new or very clean terra cotta flower pots to bake in. If you use previously used pots, run them through the dishwasher before use.

☆ Bake cupcakes in ice cream cones. Not sugar cones but the cake cones with the flat bottoms. Just make a box cake via the directions on the box then, instead of pouring it into paper cup cake holders pour the batter into ice cream cones. Place standing up on a cookie sheet, bake as directed, then frost.

**Cookie Cutter Toast:** This is a really easy "cooking" activity. Give your children each a piece of sandwich bread. This would be a good thing to do with the last few pieces of bread in the loaf. Let them cut out "cookie" shapes with cookie cutters.

Now toast the bread and "decorate." Your children can "decorate" with butter and jam, cream cheese (to add a flare of color add food coloring to the cream cheese), cinnamon sugar, peanut butter, honey. If you want to get really fancy, let them use cake frosting. You can also let your children use the cookie cutters on french toast. Yum! Yum!

✂ _Supplies You Will Need_ ✂
- ☆ Sandwich bread.
- ☆ Cookie cutters.
- ☆ Decorations.

☺ _Ways to Expand this Activity_ ☺
- ☆ Correspond the cookie cutter shape to a holiday and tint the cream cheese the appropriate color (hearts for Valentine's Day with red/pink cream cheese, Shamrocks and green cream cheese for St. Patrick's Day, and so on throughout the year).
- ☆ Use alphabet, number and/or shape cookie cutters to make this a "learning" activity.
- ☆ Let your children swirl two different colors of cream cheese together to make a new color, then discuss how it changed color.
- ☆ Your children could also "decorate" their toast with raisins, chocolate chips, small pieces of cut up dried fruit, nuts and/or popcorn.
- ☆ Let your children melt matching shapes of sliced cheese on top of the bread.

Dinosaur Eggs: This is a wonderful activity for children who are really into dinosaurs. They are sure to get a real kick out of this one. Even if your children are not particularly interested in dinosaurs at this time, this activity will excite them. Who knows, this may spark a real interest in the ancient creatures.

Instead of just dyeing the outside egg shell, with this activity you can dye the *inside* of the hard-boiled egg. First, you will need to hard-boil four eggs. Let the eggs cool for a couple of hours in the refrigerator before moving to the next step. Then, **very gently** crack the shells by tapping them on a counter top or tapping them with the back of a spoon, but don't take the shell off.

Now, in a bowl deep enough to cover your eggs with liquid, mix a package of Kool-Aid soft drink mix with enough water to completely cover the eggs. Add your cracked eggs to the colored water and cover the bowl with plastic wrap. Put your eggs in the refrigerator for one or two days. After a couple of days, take your eggs out of the refrigerator and peel off the shell. The egg on the inside of the shell will be decorated with a colored marble pattern. It will look like a dinosaur egg! It will also be mildly flavored grape, cherry, berry, or whichever flavor Kool-Aid you used.

✂ *Supplies You Will Need* ✂

☆ Four hard-boiled eggs. Even children who don't like eggs may want in on this activity!

☆ A small deep bowl.

☆ One envelope unsweetened soft drink mix.

☆ Water.

☺ *Ways to Expand this Activity* ☺

☆ Mix two different flavors (colors)of Kool-Aid together to produce a new color.

☆ Use plain food coloring to expand your choices of colors.

Dyeing Eggs: Yes, dyeing eggs. You don't have to wait until Easter to dye eggs. Your children will get just as big a kick out of it on any other day of the year as well. I'm certain most everyone already knows how to do this but, just in case here is what you do.

To make the "dye," add a tablespoon of vinegar to a cup of _hot_ water then add some food coloring. For darker dye add more food coloring, for pastel dye add a smaller amount of food coloring. Submerge the hard-boiled eggs into the dye for a few minutes and remove. Now, of course, your children will want to eat them immediately. This may be a good way to get your children to eat eggs if they normally don't like eggs.

✄ _Supplies You Will Need_ ✄

☆ Hard-boiled eggs.

☆ Water.

☆ Vinegar.

☆ Food coloring.

☺ _Ways to Expand this Activity_ ☺

☆ Let your children decorate the eggs by applying the food coloring solution with an eye dropper and spreading it around with watercolor paintbrushes.

☆ Dry Kool-aid is great for decorating eggs. Sprinkle unsweetened Kool-aid onto <u>wet</u> eggs and use watercolor paintbrushes to paint the eggs. Use empty spice jars as sprinklers.

☆ Let your children draw on the eggs with crayon before dyeing them. The wax from the crayon will prevent the dye from coloring the eggshell and they will have a neat design.

☆ Make egg salad sandwiches with the eggs after you have dyed them and opened them up.

☆ Make deviled eggs. Let your children do the mashing with a potato masher or pastry blender.

☆ Have an egg hunt. You don't have to "_call_" it an "Easter Egg Hunt" if it is not Easter time. Calling it an egg hunt will work fine. Your children will love it just the same!

Eggs in a Frame: Here is a meal in itself. An egg and toast cooked all at one time. Start with a regular slice of buttered sandwich bread. Cut a circle out of the middle of the bread with an upside down juice glass. Put the bread with the hole in it (and the hole) into a warm frying pan. Break an egg into the hole in the bread. Cook the egg, the bread and the round bread cutout (the hole) until the egg is thoroughly cooked. It is all right to turn the egg/bread over, once the egg has started to firm up, it will not fall apart on you. Now, you have an "Egg in a Frame." Yum! Yum!

The round cutout makes a fun piece of "toast" to have with the egg in a frame. Spread jam or honey or sprinkle cinnamon sugar on it, whichever suits your children's fancy.

✂ *Supplies You Will Need* ✂

- ☆ Eggs (fertile eggs are better for your family's cholesterol level).
- ☆ Buttered sandwich bread.
- ☆ Frying pan.

☺ *Ways to Expand this Activity* ☺

- ☆ Use shaped cookie cutters again and make different kinds of shapes in the bread before putting the egg into it.
- ☆ For a real change of pace, try different flavored bread: cinnamon, French bread, even pumpernickel (well maybe). At the bakery in my neighborhood grocery store they sell vividly colored sandwich bread. This makes an especially neat egg in a frame.

Food Fun . . .

Food can be a terrific source of entertainment to children. Here are several food related ideas that are not really cooking projects but, they fall under the "food" category.

Muffin tins make fun "plates" for children. If you have any finicky eaters this may work as a way to get a little more food into them. Serve your children their lunch in muffin tins. They will get a kick out of "eating out of the compartments." They may even eat more than on a normal plate day. Your local thrift store would be a good resource for muffin tins so that you have enough for everybody.

Following the muffin tin theme, let your children drink their beverage out of measuring cups or plastic champagne glasses if you have any around. They'll get a kick out of it.

Most children like sliced cheese. For fun let your children cut shapes out of the squares with cookie cutters. You can also let them cut shapes out of tortillas with cookie cutters (you will need metal ones with a cutting edge to work on the tortillas). A pizza cutter is another fun utensil to use with cheese and tortillas. If you are concerned about giving your children pizza cutters for fear they will cut themselves with the sharp edge, there are plastic pizza cutters available.

Toothpicks are another fun utensil, especially the fancy ones with colored cellophane on the top. I have gotten more food into my own son using toothpicks than any other utensil. I just cut everything into small chunks and let him pick away. He loves it and I love that he is actually eating!

Dippin'. . . children like to "dip" things into sauce. Give them unusual combinations to dip. Pretzels, celery sticks, apples (or any fruit), rice cakes into yogurt or crackers, popcorn, toasted tortillas into thinned out peanut butter or breadsticks into spaghetti sauce. Bananas dipped into chocolate pudding is especially tasty! Yum!

Frozen fruit–Frozen banana and frozen grapes are fabulous. They are healthy, and children love them to begin with, but after they are frozen they become an extra special treat. Try freezing other fruits and you may stumble on a new family favorite.

Colored ice cubes are always a kick. Fill ice cube trays with water and food coloring. The ice cubes can be all one color or several different colors depending on how you want to do it. After they are frozen, let your children have them in a drink or just let them play with them on the table. If you don't have a table with a surface that can get *that* wet, put the ice cubes in a big tray or on a cookie sheet. Mix in some salt and see what happens. Keep an eye out for novelty ice cube trays; footballs, alphabet letters, stars etc. Fun ice cube trays make great stocking stuffers. Fun and science all in one.

Use novelty ice cube trays as jello molds for extra fun (ordinary ice cube trays work too). Fun! Fun! Fun! Spray with no stick cooking spray before adding jello. Soak in warm water for 15 seconds prior to removing from molds.

Fruit Pops: Don't pay $4.00 a box for fruit *juice* popsicles when you can make your own for a third the price and it's not just juice it's fruit. Puree a 32 oz. can of pears then pour the puree into popsicle molds (you can use measuring cups as molds). Freeze overnight and have a *cool* snack the next day. This works with peaches and apricots too. Stock up on canned fruit when it goes on sale.

✄ *Supplies You Will Need* ✄

☆ Canned fruit.

☆ Popsicle molds.

☺ *Ways to Expand this Activity* ☺

☆ If you have a juicer, "juice" fresh fruit and put it into the popsicle molds. Watermelon juice is out of this world! This is a wonderful treat in the summer time too!

☆ If you don't have any popsicle molds on hand you can put the fruit/fruit juice into ice cube trays or dixie cups and use toothpicks or popsicle sticks for handles. To make the handles stand up properly, put a piece of plastic wrap over the ice cube tray or cups. Poke the handles through the plastic wrap into the fruit. The fruit will freeze with the handles standing up in place.

☆ Pudding pops are always a big hit too. Make jello pudding the way you normally would but, put it into the popsicle molds while it is still warm and workable, then freeze.

☆ You can make "special colored" pudding pops by using vanilla pudding and food coloring. For even more fun add raisins, sprinkles, mini chocolate chips, etc.

☆ Make smoothie pops! Fruit smoothies frozen in popsicle molds make smoothie pops. Smoothie pops and smoothies are a fabulous way to sneak nutrition into your children. You can add all sorts of extra nutritious things without your children being any wiser.

☆ Yogurt pops are another great way to let your children have some fun and also get some nutrition into them at the same time. My son loves yogurt pops for breakfast!

Green Eggs and Ham: Do you have the Dr. Seuss book _Green Eggs and Ham_? Have you ever considered <u>really</u> making green eggs and ham for your children? Just think what a kick your children would get out of really eating green eggs and ham.

✂ **_Supplies You Will Need_** ✂
- ☆ Eggs and green food coloring.
- ☆ Ham (diced would be nice). Let your children do the dicing.

☺ **_Ways to Expand this Activity_** ☺
- ☆ Use other colors instead of green the next time you make scrambled eggs.
- ☆ Make pink eggs on Valentines Day, green on St. Patrick's Day, pastel blue on Easter etc.

A MOMMY TIP

Give Yourself a Break! On rainy days plan to eat finger food for daytime meals (sandwiches, crackers and cut up fruit/vegetables) and plan one pot dishes for dinner meals, AND eat on paper plates the whole day. Dishes are always such a big chore added to the day. On a rainy day, if you take them out of the equation, you are one step ahead!

Have a Picnic: Eat lunch in the family room, in your children's bedroom or even out in the garage with the door up so you can watch the rain. Do the whole bit, pack a blanket and special food in a basket. You might have some special homemade treat (from a recipe in this book). If you are eating in the family room, turn a nature program on the television to make it seem more like you are really on a picnic.

✂ *Supplies You Will Need* ✂

- ☆ A picnic basket.
- ☆ Lunch, including something special for an extra special treat.
- ☆ A blanket and a lawn umbrella (set up the umbrella just for fun).

☺ *Ways to Expand this Activity* ☺

- ☆ If your children happened to have made a "fort" earlier in the day, eat in the fort. See page 34 for fort making ideas.
- ☆ Have your children help make the lunch by spreading their own peanut butter, mayo or stirring the cheese sauce into macaroni and cheese, whatever they can do to help.

MOMMY TIP

Check out page 154. You will find a complete list of all the supplies and materials needed to complete any of the activities in this book. It was devised to allow you to photocopy it and carry a copy in your purse or wallet. Then, with your list at your fingertips you will be able to pick up assorted items the next time you go to the grocery store, hardware store or craft store.

Jello Jigglers: Children love Jello Jigglers! Follow the "Jigglers" directions on the back of a box of jello. After the jello has set up, cut out shapes and let your children devour the shapes. YUM! YUM! What fun!!!

✂ *Supplies You Will Need* ✂
- ☆ One 6 oz. box of jello mix (any flavor).
- ☆ 9 x 13 in. glass baking dish.
- ☆ Cookie cutters to cut shapes out of the hardened jello.

☺ *Ways to Expand this Activity* ☺
- ☆ Add fun things to the jello (marshmallow bits, cottage cheese, applesauce, cake decorating sprinkles, <u>gummy worms</u>☺, etc.).
- ☆ Make red jello for Valentine's Day and cut out heart shapes to eat, green for St. Patrick's Day and cut out shamrocks to eat, and so on throughout the year.
- ☆ Cut letters/numbers out of the jello.
- ☆ Fill a thoroughly washed balloon, rubber glove or plastic eggs with jello.
- ☆ Add food coloring to the hot water to make the jello a different color (blue food coloring and red jello makes purple jello, yellow food coloring and red jello makes orange jello). Then, discuss colors, <u>why</u> does blue and red make purple.
- ☆ Put the jello into a jello mold or a cake mold.
- ☆ Use novelty ice cube trays (footballs, stars, etc.) as jello molds. Spray with no stick cooking spray before adding jello. Soak in warm water for 15 seconds prior to removing from molds.
- ☆ A sugar free way to make jello jigglers is to use fruit juice instead of the dry jello mix. I found this idea on the back of the Knox gelatine box. Use four packets of gelatine to 4 cups of fruit juice. Mix the gelatine with 1 cup of cold juice. Wait one minute then add 3 cups of boiling juice. Stir and chill until firm.

Pancake Magic: **This is a pretty simple idea. Add food coloring to your pancake batter. This can be one of those "special days" type of activity. Add red food coloring on Valentine's Day, green on St. Patrick's Day, pink and green "swirled" on Easter. To "swirl" the colors, separate the batter into two bowls and add different food coloring to each bowl. Pour each color batter right next to the other to form one pancake, then with a spoon gently "swirl" the colors together.**

Of course you don't have to wait for a "special" day to do this with your children. Your children will love it any day of the year. When your children are beginning to learn their colors this would be a way to help them learn.

✂ *Supplies You Will Need* ✂

☆ **Pancake mix or batter from scratch.**

☆ **Food coloring.**

☺ *Ways to Expand this Activity* ☺

☆ **Here is one of my personal favorites! A very neat way to cook pancakes is to use a turkey baster to "pour" the batter into the pan. With a turkey baster you can make just about any letter, number, shape you want. My son and I have had lots of fun with this and he can now recognize about half of the letters in the alphabet. He's not even three. What better way to learn your letters and numbers than to eat your way through, one letter/number at a time!**

☆ **Pancake molds are a lot of fun too. You can buy special pancake molds at specialty bake shops or you can use what you have around the house like metal cookie cutters or make your own molds from aluminum foil.**

☆ **This activity idea is especially fun when your children have friends over. Particularly when your children are having a sleep over. For breakfast, the next morning, spell each child's name out of pancake batter. Your children's friends will think you are the best mom in town with your talent for making colored letter pancakes. What fabulous memories!**

☆ Pancakes don't have to only be for breakfast. They make a great afternoon snack and your children will probably get a kick out of making them in the afternoon. We made lots and lots of pancakes at the preschool. It's always a favorite and the children never tire of this activity!

☆ Another fun thing to do with pancakes (and French toast) is to add special flavoring like almond (check flavors at the grocery store). If you don't want to add artificial flavoring, you can add cinnamon, shredded apple, mashed banana, blueberries, or mini chocolate chips for a change of pace. My son's favorite pancake recipe is oatmeal, cinnamon and shredded apple. To make apple-oatmeal pancakes just make a few substitutions to any pancake recipe.

To make apple-oatmeal pancakes from scratch; powderize oatmeal in your blender and use half oatmeal and half flour in place of all-purpose flour. Add the rest of the ingredients called for in your recipe (except the apple) to a blender and give it a whirl. Hand stir in the apple after everything else is blended, then pour onto hot griddle, cook, and eat. YUM!

Basic pancake recipe:

1 egg
1 cup all-purpose flour
¾ c. milk
2 T. vegetable oil
1 T. sugar, maple syrup or honey
3 tsp. baking powder
½ tsp. salt

Mix all ingredients together, pour onto hot griddle, cook and enjoy!

Peanut Butter: This is an easy activity. Your children will probably get a kick out of making their own peanut butter. Even if your children don't like peanut butter, this will be "special" peanut butter. They may enjoy this activity anyway and they may even eat some peanut butter when ordinarily they wouldn't touch the stuff. All you do is grind up about a cup or so of peanuts in your blender. Add a small amount of oil to make it smooth and maybe a touch of honey, but that's it. Easy! For best results—let your children do everything, shell the peanuts (of course, pre-shelled peanuts will work too but, the "shelling" process will help keep your children happy and entertained for a while), put the peanuts into the blender, start the blender and spread the peanut butter themselves.

✂ ***Supplies You Will Need*** ✂
- ☆ Unsalted peanuts in the shell (salt to taste after it is blended).
- ☆ Vegetable oil (cold-pressed vegetable oil is the healthiest for you).
- ☆ Honey (optional).

☺ ***Ways to Expand this Activity*** ☺
- ☆ Instead of just peanut buttering bread, eat some with celery, toasted English muffins, pancakes, french toast, waffles, tortillas, graham crackers or any cracker for that matter, rice cakes, bagels, pita bread, apples, bananas (peanut butter and banana sandwiches are very popular with some people).
- ☆ Let your children use cookie cutters to cut fun shapes out of the bread/pancakes/tortillas then spread peanut butter on the shapes.
- ☆ You can make almond butter from almonds too. If your children like almonds they may also really enjoy almond butter. Make almond butter the same way you would make peanut butter.

Personal Pizzas: I'm sure you're quite familiar with this activity. It seems everybody makes pizza with their children, but just in case, I decided to throw it in. When you need an idea, and fast, this idea could just fill the bill! You have a lot of options with this activity.

Crust ideas: Homemade dough, sliced bread, English muffins, hamburger or hot dog buns, French bread or even tortillas.

Sauce ideas: Plain tomato sauce with a few spices sprinkled on top (garlic, basil, oregano and Parmesan cheese). Spaghetti sauce right out of the jar, pizza sauce out of the jar, barbecue sauce, pesto sauce or even ranch dressing makes a pretty good sauce.

Topping ideas: Any combination of cheeses you like (whatever you have available in the fridge). Of course, pepperoni is a favorite but, I recommend only eating it occasionally. Pepperoni, and all processed lunchmeat, contain Sodium Nitrate which is a cancer causing preservative. UGH! Try "different" toppings: leftover chicken chunks, pineapple, sundried tomatoes, olives, etc.

✂ **_Supplies You Will Need_** ✂

☆ Something to use as a crust. Lot of ideas listed above.

☆ Sauce & toppings.

☆ Plastic pizza cutters. Children just love to use pizza cutters.

☺ **_Ways to Expand this Activity_** ☺

☆ Here's a twist on the Mexican quesadillas. My Dad came up with this combination when I was a young child. On a flour tortilla, spread a tablespoon or two of ketchup. Top with cheddar and monterey jack cheese (mixed), then bake in a 350° oven until the cheese melts. This was one of my favorite lunches as a child and now it is one of my son's favorite meals. Yum! Yum!

Popcorn Soup: Here is an idea from my own childhood. My mother used to put popcorn (popped of course) into our split pea soup so that my sister and I would eat it. This is the same idea as oyster crackers. You don't have to be limited to just split pea soup. You can put popcorn into any kind of soup just for fun. Your children may even ask for seconds, wouldn't that be great.

✂ *Supplies You Will Need* ✂

☆ Any kind of soup will work, but a thick soup (split pea, clam chowder, tomato, etc.) will suspend the popcorn longer than a noodles and broth type of soup.

☆ Add canned, frozen or baby corn to the soup and discuss with your children the different type of corn (popped versus not popped).

☆ Cornbread muffins are another "corn thing" to include. You might talk about how corn kernels are ground up into flour to make cornmeal and then into cornbread.

☺ *Ways to Expand this Activity* ☺

☆ Here's a brave idea—pop your popcorn with the lid off! Sounds wild doesn't it? Believe it or not, I have actually done this. As you can imagine, children get an incredible thrill out of it. The best way to do this is to spread out a large sheet on the floor and put and electric skillet in the middle. Add a <u>tiny</u> bit of oil and spread it around the skillet with a paper towel. <u>Too much oil will splatter!</u> Add a small amount of popcorn, turn up the heat and watch the action! It's a BLAST!

☆ Make "baby" dumplings and add to your children's soup.

☆ Add broken up crackers, pretzels or corn chips to soup.

☆ Let your children cut shapes out of wonton wrappers with cookie cutters or a pizza cutter and add to their soup. Bring the soup up to a boil for a few minutes after adding the wonton wrappers so they can cook thoroughly. Oh, What Fun!!!

Sugar and Spice: If you are not a cook, you will like this activity, no cooking involved. Children love to explore their five senses. Here is an activity for the nose. Open up your spice rack and let the sniffing begin. In other words, let your children explore the many different smells and tastes in your spice collection. It may seem strange to let your children taste plain, dry basil or oregano, but children love to explore new things, including spices and flavorings. Furthermore, most children will not be content with just smelling the spices, they will be curious and will want to taste everything too (exclude cayenne, onion and black pepper).

Put several different spices/seasonings into different paper muffin cups. Let your children smell each paper cup. See if they can guess what spice/seasoning they are smelling, then let them taste each one. Which one do they like the best? Does one certain spice remind them of a particular food (pizza or chili)? For liquid seasonings, put a few drops (peppermint or almond etc.) onto a cotton ball and into the paper cups. If this seems like an activity that your children will want to play with for a few days, put the scented cotton balls into plastic film containers. Punch a few holes in the tops of the film containers and the scent will last for a few days. The film container idea (or some similar container with a lid) can be used for more than just spices. Try different perfumes, rose petals and other flowers, pine needles, juice or the rind from an orange, lemon or other fragrant fruit, fresh mint, toothpaste etc. There are dozens of smells available around your house.

✄ **_Supplies You Will Need_** ✄
- ☆ Just your spices. Of course, stay away from the hot spices.
- ☆ Paper muffin cups.
- ☆ Empty film, spice or pill containers with the lids.

☺ **_Ways to Expand this Activity_** ☺
- ☆ Add a matching game to this activity by drawing pictures of what is in the containers and see if your children can match the correct smell with the pictures.

Toast Art: Let your children be artistic at lunch time. With this activity your children can "paint" on white sandwich bread with milk and food coloring. In three or four small bowls, mix milk and food coloring together. Each bowl is a different color. Now, give your children _new_ watercolor paintbrushes and let them "paint" a design on their bread and toast it.

✀ _Supplies You Will Need_ ✀

☆ White sandwich bread, wheat will work but, the design shows up better on white bread.

☆ Milk.

☆ Food coloring.

☆ _New_ watercolor paintbrushes, you can usually buy them at the grocery store for about a dollar a package.

☺ _Ways to Expand this Activity_ ☺

☆ You can use flour tortillas, hamburger or hot dog buns, or a slice of pound cake instead of bread.

☆ Another way to be artistic on toast is to sprinkle colored sugar on top of the bread, just as if you were sprinkling colored sugar onto sugar cookies. This work really well if the toast is spread with cream cheese first.

☆ You can make stencils from paper plates to hold over the toast before sprinkling on the colored sugar. Now, your children will have a design on their toast.

MEASURING, SIFTING, SORTING & STRINGING

Sandbox play—INDOORS?

Do your children love to play in the sandbox? Most children do and would stay in the sandbox all day if you would let them. The following group of activities give your children the "sandbox" experience, but indoors. These activities are all very open-ended and really allow your children to "get into it up to their elbows." These are some of the old standbys in the preschool setting due to their favoriteness. They are the silver medalist of the book!

Your children will benefit educationally as well, as sandbox type play (measuring and sifting) will help your children begin to develop math concepts (how many 1 cup measuring cups does it take to fill up a juice pitcher). These activities aid in developing, or fine tuning if you will, your children's sensory systems (touch, smell, taste) and also hand-eye coordination.

Beans, Beans: For some reason children really love to play with dried beans. It must be because the beans feel so neat to run your fingers through and are so interesting to look at up close. Give your children a big tub, a few pounds of beans in it, some kitchen utensils, and watch the fun.

✂ Supplies You Will Need ✂

☆ A large tray or tub. Wal Mart has a large Rubbermaid® plastic "under the bed" storage bin for $4.97. It's perfect for the indoor sandbox type of activities. Any large box will do though.

☆ A few pounds of dried pinto beans, kidney beans, black eyed peas, whatever.

☆ Kitchen utensils: measuring cups and spoons, funnels, plastic plates etc.

☺ Ways to Expand this Activity ☺

☆ After your children have had plenty of playing time, you might interrupt this activity to take out a few beans for sprouting.

Sprouting . . . a couple of different ways to "sprout" beans are: Put a half dozen or so beans into a zip lock bag with a few moist cotton balls. Next, set the beans on a warm window sill (out of direct sunlight) for a couple of days. Or another way would be to put your beans onto a clean meat tray with moist paper towels covering them. Either way in a few days you should see the beans begin to split open and roots will appear. Then, if you are so inclined, you could plant the beans and watch them grow. To take this activity even further you could read <u>Jack and the Bean Stalk.</u>

<u>A word of caution though;</u> make sure that when your children are finished you picked up every single last bean which has fallen onto the floor. Otherwise, the second you are not looking, your children will find a stray bean and find an opening to insert it into like their nose or ear. Once in the nose, if moisture hits the bean, it will begin to swell making it very difficult to remove without the help of a doctor and the proper instrument. I suggest discussing this hazard with your children.

Cornmeal Sandbox: This is an easy one, and relatively clean. The cornmeal cleans up easily with the vacuum. Put cornmeal and several kitchen gadgets into a container that you have chosen and let your children go to town.

Be prepared for a "pretend" feast. Your children will make you cake, pie, pizza, hamburgers, milkshakes and whatever else their imagination cooks up. It's wonderful fun! What is this activity good for besides keeping them busy while you're on the phone, mending, folding laundry etc.? Well, lots, this activity gets your children's imagination going. Creative imagination is very important for proper brain development. When children use their imagination they are developing "thinking" and problem solving skills. This activity also helps develop hand-eye coordination and small motor skills. It also helps to develop math skills. For example, how many measuring cup scoops does it take to fill up the plastic bowl?

This is also a sensory activity. What that means is, children love to explore their five senses and this activity stimulates their sense of touch. Running their fingers and hands through the cornmeal is a neat feeling. In fact, before you give your children any utensils just let them play with the cornmeal by itself for a little while.

To prevent your cornstarch or other "sandbox food" from an insect infestation, put a ziplock bag filled with rock salt in the container when not in use. I don't know how this works, but it does. I just got about a cup of rock salt out of our water softener and that has worked great. However you can buy rock salt in the salt section at the grocery store if you do not have a water softener. This will work in your kitchen cabinets too. Put a bag of rock salt in your cabinet with your flour, other baking ingredients and/or grains. As far as I know you do not need rock salt in every container. As long as there is rock salt in close proximity to flour or grains, it will keep the bugs away.

✄ *Supplies You Will Need* ✄

☆ A large tray of some kind. See page 91 under "supplies you will need."

☆ A couple of 5 lb. bags of cornmeal.

☆ Most of your kitchen gadgets (measuring cups & spoons, funnels, little plastic bowls & lids, spatula's, garlic presses, a sifter, etc.).

☆ A large zip lock bag. Store the cornmeal in a large zip lock bag when not in use.

☺ *Ways to Expand this Activity* ☺

☆ Let your children play in the cornmeal with little figurines (like the little toys that come in Happy Meals). At the thrift shop in my neighborhood they have a large basket in the back of the store overflowing with those little characters. Instead of spending a fortune at the fast food restaurants check out your local thrift shop. Your children can probably get ten toys for the price of one.

☆ Let your children play with small cars, trucks, trains and/or plastic animals. They might make a town or farm. See what their imagination cooks up.

Note: This activity is a keeper. Put a lid on the cornmeal container and save it for another day. The cornmeal will keep forever as long as it doesn't get wet.

☆ Add a small amount of powdered paint to the cornmeal to make colored cornmeal.

Rainbow Rice: This activity might be a little expensive but, it is a neat one and the rice will last forever. Buy two or three 10 lb. bags of rice. Divide the rice into two, three, or four piles. Color each pile of rice a different color with the food coloring and rubbing alcohol solution (instructions are on the next page). When it is dry, mix all the rice together in large tray. You will have a beautiful rainbow of rice for your children to feel, scoop, and measure. Your children will love it!!!

✄ _Supplies You Will Need_ ✄

☆ Colored rice. You really don't have to color it, plain white rice will do just fine.

☆ A large tray of some kind. See page 91 under "supplies you will need."

☆ Kitchen utensils: measuring cups & spoons, funnels, plastic bowls, spatulas etc.

☆ A large zip lock bag. Store the rice in a large zip lock bag when not in use.

☺ _Ways to Expand this Activity_ ☺

☆ Use some of the rice for gluing onto paper and/or paper plates.

☆ Make colored rice and have it with lunch. <u>Use new rice,</u> not the rice that has rubbing alcohol on it. The way to make edible colored rice is to make rice the regular way (two parts water to one part rice) and add a small amount (¼–½ tsp.) of food coloring. If you are concerned about your children eating too much food coloring, you can buy natural food coloring in a heath food store.

☆ The colored rice idea can be used on special holiday days to go with the theme of the day (pink for Valentine's Day, green for St. Patrick's Day, orange on Halloween etc.).

To Color Rice

Mix a 16 oz. bottle of rubbing alcohol and 1 tsp. of food coloring (any color) together in a bowl. An aluminum pie tin works really well. I would suggest using something metal or something that you won't care if it gets stained by the food coloring. <u>Don't use your favorite Tupperware bowl for this project.</u> I have not had a problem with staining but just to be on the safe side use caution.

Submerge as much rice into the rubbing alcohol solution as will fit for 1 to 2 min. Drain off the rubbing alcohol (you can save the alcohol solution right in the bottle it came in for another batch on another day).

Now spread the rice out onto paper plates or paper towels to absorb the excess rubbing alcohol solution. Let dry overnight on the paper plates or paper towels. In the morning you will have beautiful rice for your children to mix and measure with.

To Color Macaroni

You can color macaroni in the exact same way you colored the rice. Use any kind of macaroni and follow the same directions for coloring rice. When the macaroni drys your children can use it to string necklaces or glue colored macaroni on paper or any number of creative uses.

Sifting Flour and Rice: Your children can play with the flour and rice the same as they would with the cornmeal except add a strainer, the kind with fine wire mesh. Let them "sift" the rice out of the flour.

This activity may require more effort in the clean up department. The flour is so lightweight that it becomes airborne very easily; therefore, you may want to closely supervise this activity for the first few sessions to make sure your rules are well understood. Even if you do end up with a nice little mess, it cleans up easily with a vacuum. Avoid water, otherwise you will have quite a different sort of mess to deal with, very sticky goo.

✄ **_Supplies You Will Need_** ✄

☆ A large tray of some kind. See page 91 under "supplies you will need."

☆ A 5 lb. bag of flour and a cup or two of rice.

☆ Kitchen utensils: especially important is a sifter, plus add measuring spoons & cups, plastic bowls, funnels, a strainer etc.

☆ A large zip lock bag. Store the flour in a large zip lock bag when not in use.

☺ **_Ways to Expand this Activity_** ☺

☆ You can add dried beans to the flour instead of rice and/or glitter and/or confetti or all of the above and have a smorgasbord of things in the flour.

☆ You can add a little dry tempra paint to the flour to color it and/or add a cup or two of colored dry rice.

Sorting Stuff: This is a good activity for a child who has good concentration skills or you might use this as an activity to *build* good concentration skills. This activity is probably best suited for children to do one at a time. Give your child different things to sort. Beans and Fruit Loops are really good for sorting. An egg carton or an ice cube tray makes a good holder for the sorted items. Sorting is a good activity for helping to develop organizational skills and sequential thinking abilities.

✂ *Supplies You Will Need* ✂

- ☆ Beans. Bean soup mixes that are available in the pasta/bean section of your supermarket work well for this activity. They come prepackaged with several different type of beans in them just waiting to be sorted. Remember to pick up every last bean if you use them for this activity (see page 91).
- ☆ Fruit Loops or mix a couple of different kinds of macaroni together and let your child separate the macaroni.
- ☆ An ice cube tray or an egg carton.

☺ *Ways to Expand this Activity* ☺

- ☆ Other things to sort: buttons, colored paper clips, beads, nuts and bolts, M&M's. There are lots and lots of possibilities available.
- ☆ This idea is for older children. If you don't have any beans or Fruit Loops around, then you could just give your child some Cheerios or macaroni and have them put, first one (Cheerio) in each compartment, then two, then three and so on. This is the beginning of math skills.

Sorting - More Ideas: This time use muffin tins. Your children will be able to sort larger things like little plastic colored teddy bears or poker chips by color. Caps are great for sorting. Start saving caps and lids to things like medicine bottle tops, plastic milk bottle tops, juice can lids, film container lids, salad dressing tops etc. When you have collected a good size group of caps (which shouldn't take too long), then your children can either sort the caps out from each other (medicine caps go with medicine caps and coke bottle tops go with coke bottle tops etc.) or you can make the caps more distinguishable by labeling them in some way. Paint the caps/lids different colors. Put stickers on them with four or five of them all having the same sticker. Write numbers or letters on the caps/lids or any other way you can think of to separate them in some way. Now, you have a sorting game that didn't cost a dime.

✄ _Supplies You Will Need_ ✄

☆ A muffin tin, this may be a good item to pick up at your local thrift store, if you would rather not have your children use yours.

☆ Something to sort (ideas listed above).

☆ A large zip lock bag. Store your sorting pieces in a large zip lock bag.

☺ _Ways to Expand this Activity_ ☺

☆ If your children are sorting by color you can cut out different color circles of paper (or white paper with different color X's or smiley faces etc. on them). Then, your children can sort the items into the appropriate spots.

☆ Other things to sort: any game or toy (Lego's, Bristle blocks or snap together toys) that have small different colored pieces can be sorted.

Stringing Cheerios: _You_ will love this one as well as your children. Children _love_ to string things! Besides, Cheerios don't make much of a mess, if at all, and if they do it is very easy to clean up. So easy, that if a few Cheerios do end up on the floor, your children can easily clean them up by themselves with a small dust pan and little broom (it may take some practice to "effectively" get them cleaned up, but practice makes perfect). This activity doesn't require very much supervision. You might be able to actually get something done while your children are busy with this one.

Cut some yarn or string into the length of a necklace or bracelet or both. Wrap the end of the yarn or string with masking tape so that the end won't become frayed. You might also have your children use a plastic tapestry needle or tape a toothpick to the string to use as a needle. Next, tie a Cheerio to the other end of the string to stop the rest of the Cheerios from falling off of the end of the string. Then, let your children go to town. It may take them anywhere from five minutes to (hopefully) an hour to make their necklace. This activity helps develop hand-eye coordination and small muscle development in their hands.

Note: This is a good activity for the end of the day when you are trying to get dinner on the table and your children are apt to be hungry, tired and crabby. It will help keep them busy and happy for a while and they can eat the Cheerios as they go. Cheerios won't spoil their dinner.

✂ _Supplies You Will Need_ ✂

☆ A box of Cheerios or the cheaper store brand of Toasted O's and/or a box of Fruit Loops.

☆ Some yarn or string.

☆ Masking tape, plastic tapestry needle or toothpick to use as a needle.

☺ _Ways to Expand this Activity_ ☺

☆ There's plenty of things to string; buttons, straws cut into one inch length, beads, macaroni.

☆ Use red vine licorice (the long thin rope type) instead of string and make a "totally" edible necklace with the Cheerios or Fruit Loops.

Stringing & Lacing: **This activity may require some assistance in the beginning, especially if your children are under four years old. At any craft store you can purchase plastic needles that don't have very sharp points. Your children can string a necklace from popcorn or Kiks cereal.**

Thread the needle with a thick piece of thread. Then, show your children how to thread the popcorn and/or cereal onto the needle and thread. Once they get going and get the hang of it they may be busy for quite a while.

Your children will also be able to do lacing activities with the plastic needle. Thread the needle with yarn and give your children a paper plate that has holes punched out around the rim. Let them thread/lace the yarn through the holes. Once they get the hang of it, you can give them two paper plates with holes punched out and they can lace the paper plates together (rim to rim). These are good activities for developing hand-eye coordination and concentration skills.

✄ ***Supplies You Will Need*** ✄

☆ **Plastic needles, called tapestry needles, can be purchased at any craft/fabric store.**

☆ **String and/or yarn.**

☆ **Things to string; popcorn, Kiks cereal, buttons, beads, straws etc.**

☆ **Things to lace; paper plates, cardboard, manila folders, cut up cereal boxes (cut up cereal boxes work real well because you can cut them into any shape, hearts, flowers, letters, etc.).**

☺ ***Ways to Expand this Activity*** ☺

☆ **Cut a cereal box into the letters of your children's names, punch holes (randomly) in the letters and let your children lace their names. When they are all finished you can string the letters together and hang the string of letters up to show off your children's lacing skills. Your children will be so proud.**

☆ **Let your children string yarn through a styrofoam meat tray. Run meat trays through the dishwasher with a couple of tablespoons of bleach to disinfect them before use.**

Stringing Macaroni: Here is another activity that is easy to clean up and requires very little supervision. Hooray!!! Prepare the activity the same as you would to string popcorn and let your children go to town. You can even mix things up a bit. Your children can string Cheerios, Fruit Loops, macaroni and cut up drinking straws all on one string.

Color the macaroni if you would like to add pizazz to it. To color the macaroni, use the same rubbing alcohol and food coloring solution as with the rice (see page 95). Make up a bunch of colored macaroni and store it away for other rainy days to come. It stores just like regular macaroni, it won't get moldy providing it is completely dry when you put it away. Please be careful to make sure your children don't eat the macaroni that has rubbing alcohol on it. Most, if not all of the alcohol has evaporated from the macaroni but, just to be on the safe side, discuss it with your children anyway.

✂ *Supplies You Will Need* ✂

- ☆ Rigatoni or macaroni salad noodles.
- ☆ String or yarn (wrap stringing end with masking tape or have your children use a tapestry needle or a toothpick taped to the string in place of a needle).
- ☆ Miscellaneous other things to string.

☺ *Ways to Expand this Activity* ☺

- ☆ Color macaroni to correspond with an approaching holiday (red, white and blue for Fourth of July, orange and black for Halloween etc.).
- ☆ Let your children color the macaroni with watercolor felt markers.
- ☆ Add shapes cut from paper (hearts, shamrocks, Easter eggs etc.). Punch a hole in the middle of the shape so it can be added to the string.

Children need a place to "work"!

Children need a place to "work" which is *their* size and shape. You will have much greater success with the activities in this book if your children have a table and chair set that is *their* (short) size. If you don't already have a table and chair set for your children and may consider purchasing one, here are a few points to consider while you are making your decision.

<u>For starters</u> - Size: many of the children's table and chairs furniture sets available are just too small! Children are messy. They need the room to really spread out and "work." There is nothing more frustrating than being cramped for space when you are trying to work on a project (any mom who doesn't have enough counter space or dad who doesn't have enough workbench space will agree). Children feel the same way. They may stay involved in a project for a much longer time if they have ample table space. I suggest at least 24" x 36" table top surface area by 20" high, minimum, but the bigger the better.

<u>Next is location</u> - I suggest putting your children's "work" table right in the kitchen or family room (over linoleum) where you can set your children up doing a project. Then, while they are busy you can work on dinner, fold laundry or maybe even do something really daring like pay bills. WOW!

<u>Next is ease of cleaning</u> - Be sure to get a table with a tough *cleanable* finish. Children are brutal on furniture so you have to get a table that is tougher than they are. Go industrial if you can!

<u>Last is storage of supplies</u> - Your kitchen will actually stay clean if your children have a "home" for all their supplies. Stacking bins are great for this but a cabinet with plastic storage boxes is great too.

On page 153, I list a school supply company. You can order children's furniture
(designed for schools) at very reasonable prices. This way you can
get exactly the right size for your house and children.

PAINTING IDEAS

Painting is a wonderful experience for children and it can tame the wildest of children by giving them an open-ended and creative place to direct their energies. The idea of *painting in the house* may make your heart skip a beat, but it can keep your children busy for possibly hours. Surprisingly, having children paint is not as messy an activity as it may seem. After years of conducting painting activities, I can honestly say that there have been very few mishaps resulting in stained carpets (stained clothing is another story so have your children wear old clothes or smocks). A tip about using tempra paint is to add liquid dishsoap to your paint. It will come out of clothing better that way. If you do end up with paint on clothing, just pre-treat with Spray & Wash prior to sending it through the wash.

Planning can make or break you—Collect everything you will need ahead of time (paint, paper, smocks, and a place to dry your children's creations). Cover everything, the table, your children and even the floor.

Smocks are easy. You don't need a special plastic smock with cute cartoon characters on it. An old shirt of yours will do just fine. Then, when your children are finished, you can just throw the smocks into the wash with a load of towels. The paint generally washes out just fine.

<u>Clean up:</u> You will want to have a bucket of warm water and a towel nearby for messy hands. This is much easier than trying to make it down the hall to the bathroom to wash up. I know that tempra paint will come out of clothes, but I'm not sure how well it comes out of carpeting.

Finger Painting: **Most children like to finger paint. It gives them a rare opportunity to get messy. This can be a special treat, since most of the time they are being told not to get messy. Set your children up with a nice big piece of paper and a few globs of paint.**

✄ ***Supplies You Will Need*** ✄
- ☆ **Tempra paint (it does not have to be specifically "finger paint").**
- ☆ **Several large sheets of paper, the larger the better.**
- ☆ **A table covered with newspaper, a tarp, an old sheet, or whatever else you have around. You might even put your children right down on the kitchen floor.**
- ☆ **Smocks.**

☺ ***Ways to Expand this Activity*** ☺
- ☆ **Add glitter to your paint.**
- ☆ **Cut shapes or letters out of the middle of the paper. In the art world this is called negative space.**
- ☆ **Draw shapes or letters on the paper before your children begin to paint.**
- ☆ **Make the paper a funny shape.**

MOMMY TIP

Add liquid dishsoap to your tempra paint. It will come out of clothing better that way.

Gadget Painting: "Gadget" means just about anything in your house (kitchen utensils, toys, toy trucks, blocks, empty spools from your sewing box, etc.). Balloons are fun too. Be careful not to blow them up too full though, if a balloon pops with paint on it you will have quite a mess. Clean meat trays work very nicely for holding the paint with this type of activity. Let your children dip "gadgets" into the paint in the meat trays. Then, they can make "gadget" prints on their paper.

✂ _Supplies You Will Need_ ✂

☆ Gravy consistency tempra paint (add soap). If it is too runny it drips too much.

☆ Paper to paint on. Consider ideas from "ways to expand this activity" from finger painting.

☆ Various kinds of "gadgets", whatever you are willing to give up to your children for the day.

☆ Clean styrofoam meat trays for holding the paint (run them through you dishwasher with bleach).

☆ Smocks.

☺ _Ways to Expand this Activity_ ☺

☆ Food can even be used. Apples, carrots or potatoes can be cut into shapes and dipped into the paint and used to make food prints.

☆ Correspond color of paint to an approaching holiday.

☆ Don't forget cookie cutters, they make great gadget painting prints.

MOMMY TiP

A couple of Dad's old shirts with the sleeves removed make great smocks to protect your children's clothes.

Ice Painting: For this activity you will need a small block of ice. You can make a block of ice with an empty 1/2 gallon milk container, a Tupperware® jello mold, a water balloon, a bundt cake pan, muffin tins, or even a one gallon food wrap bag filled with water and put into some sort of odd shaped container (a vase).

After the water has frozen solid, pull it out of the freezer. Remove it from its container and let your children "paint" on the ice with watercolors. You can use just regular watercolors paints like the ones you can buy in the grocery store (each color has its own well). I suggest you buy an extra set of brushes. Those watercolor sets generally come with one brush and those brushes tend to lose most of their bristles during the first use.

✄ *Supplies You Will Need* ✄

☆ Ice in some form or another. Be sure to make one of the sides flat so that when you pull the ice out of its mold it won't roll around while your children are trying to paint on it. Placing a towel under the ice also helps keep it from moving around.

☆ Watercolor paints.

☆ Paintbrushes.

☺ *Ways to Expand this Activity* ☺

☆ Add things to the water before freezing (toys, flowers, kitchen utensils, etc.) the melting process will be neat for your children to watch as items slowly melt loose.

☆ Add food coloring to the water.

☆ Try filling up a rubber glove with water and freezing it. The glove should peel off of the ice but, use an old glove just in case you have to cut it off.

☆ After your children have been painting for a while and it looks like they are about ready to move on to something else, sprinkle salt on the ice. Your children will be amazed!

Marble Painting: **How do you paint with a marble? Here's how. The next time you buy a case of soda save the cardboard box that it comes in. Place a piece of paper in the bottom of the box then put a few small globs of tempra paint on the paper. Your paint needs to be about the consistency of mayonnaise. Put a marble or two into the box. Then, show your children how to wiggle and tip the box around so that the marbles roll through the paint. The marbles will make a paint trail on the paper. If you use a couple of different colors, when the paint trails cross each other, they will make a new color. Children seem to have a lot of fun with this activity.**

✄ ***Supplies You Will Need*** ✄
- ☆ **A cardboard box (any shallow box will do).**
- ☆ **Thick tempra paint.**
- ☆ **Paper that fits inside the cardboard box.**
- ☆ **Marbles.**
- ☆ **Smocks.**

☺ ***Ways to Expand this Activity*** ☺
- ☆ **Use different things to paint on like aluminum foil, sandpaper, fabric and wallpaper.**
- ☆ **Use an approaching holiday's colors and make place mats for your dinner table for that holiday. Children love to eat off placemats that they have made themselves.**
- ☆ **Make the paper different interesting shapes.**
- ☆ **Use different colored paper.**
- ☆ **Put cars in the box and make car tire tracks along with the marble tracks.**
- ☆ **Try using golf balls instead of marbles.**

Painting with Q-tips: This activity will get you out of washing paintbrushes. Let your children paint with Q-tips. When they are finished painting, just throw the Q-tips away. This is also a relatively clean activity. Your children won't be able to spread very much paint at a time. Q-tips don't hold much paint. Your children will spend most of their time dipping the Q-tip into the paint. Then, after making a couple of streaks on their paper they will have to get more paint. It will take your children some time to fill up a piece of paper with paint, and best yet, it will help keep your children happy and entertained for a while.

✄ *Supplies You Will Need* ✄
- ☆ Paint.
- ☆ Paper.
- ☆ Q-tips.
- ☆ Smocks.

☺ *Ways to Expand this Activity* ☺
- ☆ Draw something on the paper before your children start to paint (shapes, letters, numbers etc.). Then, see if your children can trace the shape.
- ☆ Let your children paint on something other than paper (cardboard boxes, paper towel rolls, cereal boxes cut open and turned inside out etc.).
- ☆ Use appropriate colors for an approaching holiday.

Rain Painting: **Here is a way to include Mother Nature in the activities. Let your children paint a piece of paper with a couple of different colors of paint and set the paper outside in the rain. The rain drops do the rest, they will make a neat pattern on the paper.**

✂ ***Supplies You Will Need*** ✂

- ☆ **Paper.**
- ☆ **Tempra paint (add soap).**
- ☆ **Rain.**
- ☆ **Paintbrushes.**

☺ ***Ways to Expand this Activity*** ☺

- ☆ **Try using wallpaper scraps or paper plates instead of regular paper.**

Crayon Resist: **On white paper have your children draw a picture with crayon (or *you* draw a mystery picture in white crayon). Next, let them paint on the paper with watercolor paints. The areas on the paper covered with crayon will not soak up the paint and it will produce a neat effect.**

✂ ***Supplies You Will Need*** ✂

- ☆ **White paper.**
- ☆ **Crayons.**
- ☆ **Watercolor paints.**
- ☆ **Smocks.**
- ☆ **Paintbrushes.**

☺ ***Ways to Expand this Activity*** ☺

- ☆ **You can use many other things besides regular white paper (paper plates, cardboard, cut up file folders, adding machine tape, grocery bags, etc.).**

Rubber Cement Resist: This time instead of crayon have your children make a design with rubber cement. You will have to wait a little while for the rubber cement to dry. Then, let your children paint with watercolor paints; the same thing will happen as with the crayon resist. The paint won't cover the rubber cement and you will have a neat effect.

✂ _Supplies You Will Need_ ✂

- ☆ Paper.
- ☆ Rubber cement.
- ☆ Watercolor paints.
- ☆ Paintbrushes.
- ☆ Smocks.

☻ _Ways to Expand this Activity_ ☻

- ☆ You can also do this activity with regular white glue but, then you have to wait for the glue to dry which takes much longer than rubber cement.

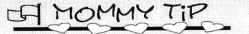

MOMMY TIP

An old shower curtain makes a great drop cloth for under messy activities and/or for covering the table you will be using.

Rock Painting: This activity takes a little planning ahead. On a "not rainy day" day, take a "field trip" out into your backyard (or neighborhood park, or a walk down the street). Have your children pick out some good size rocks (the bigger they are, the longer they take to paint). Then, on the next rainy day they can paint on them. You can even make this activity last a couple of days. After the rocks are dry your children can either draw, paint or glue "eyes" and "hair" on their rock. If your children somehow could not find any "big" rocks then maybe they could collect several smaller rocks, paint them and glue them together.

✄ **_Supplies You Will Need_** ✄
- ☆ Tempra paint (add soap).
- ☆ Paintbrushes.
- ☆ Clean rocks.
- ☆ Smocks.

☺ **_Ways to Expand this Activity_** ☺
- ☆ Let your children paint with something other than paintbrushes. Let them use Q-tips, old toothbrushes, sponges etc.

MOMMY TIP

Painting on three dimensional objects offers children a very new and different painting experience. Empty pizza boxes, cereal boxes, paper towel rolls, scrapes of wood, toilet paper rolls taped together into interesting sculptures etc. all offer ways to expand the "painting experience." Plus, it's just plain fun to slather paint all over a pizza box.

Sponge Painting: Same fun as finger painting, but a different technique. Instead of painting with their fingers your children will paint with sponges. This is a great way to recycle your old sponges. Run them through the dishwasher before retiring them to sponge painting though.

If your children don't like to get their hands messy or wet, this may be more appealing than finger painting (some children just don't like the gooey feeling on their hands). If this is even too "gooey" for your children, put clothespins on the sponges as handles.

✂ **_Supplies You Will Need_** ✂
- ☆ Tempra paint (add soap).
- ☆ Paper to paint on.
- ☆ An assortment of sponges. Cut the sponges down into smaller shapes.
- ☆ Clean styrofoam meat trays for holding the paint (run them through your dishwasher with bleach).
- ☆ Clothespins.
- ☆ Smocks.

☺ **_Ways to Expand this Activity_** ☺
- ☆ You could try to make animal shapes, numbers or letters (maybe the letters of your children's names) out of the sponges.
- ☆ Add glitter to the paint.
- ☆ Use holiday colors.
- ☆ Make the paper funny shapes.

Wet paper; Dry paint: This may seem like painting backwards but, it produces a neat effect. Fingerpaint paper probably works the best for this activity, but butcher paper or freezer paper with one shiny side will work well too. If you don't have either of those kinds of paper go ahead and use whatever you have around the house. Even the inside of a paper grocery bag will do just fine.

What you do with this activity is to first paint the paper with clear water, then sprinkle <u>dry</u> tempra paint onto the wet paper. As the dry paint hits the wet paper it begins to dissolve and turn to liquid. It is a neat reaction for children to watch. Then, after the paint has liquefied your children can "paint" as they normally would with paintbrushes.

To make "sprinklers" to sprinkle the paint, punch several holes in the bottom of a paper drinking cup with a needle or small nail. Put different colors into each cup and let your children "sprinkle a masterpiece."

✄ _Supplies You Will Need_ ✄

☆ Paper. Finger paint paper is large sheets of paper with one very shiny side. It is available through Discount School Supply listed on page 153.

☆ Dry tempra paint.

☆ Paper cups for "sprinklers." Salt shakers work well too, a good thrift shop purchase.

☆ Paintbrushes.

☺ _Ways to Expand this Activity_ ☺

☆ Add "fine" glitter to the dry paint.

☆ Try the crayon resist painting idea with this activity. Let your children draw on the paper first, then "paint" it with water.

☆ Wet the paper first then let your children use chalk instead of paint.

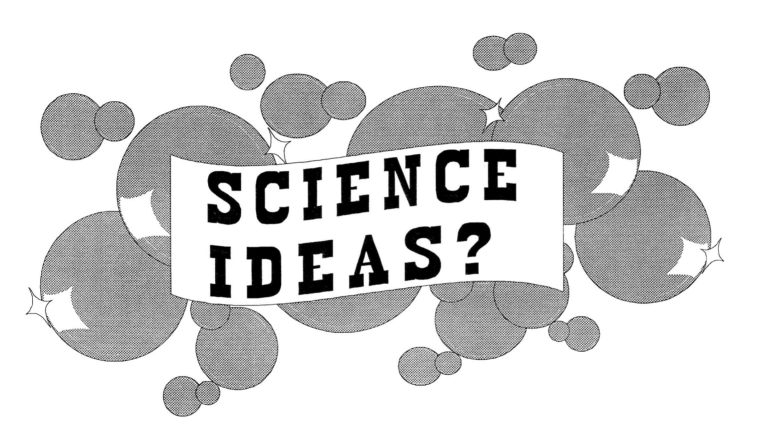

SCIENCE IDEAS?

Is There a Scientist in the House?

When I started this project, I really had not intended on making any of it "*educational.*" My plan was to put together a list of well-rounded, mainly fun, entertaining, I need a great idea NOW, group of activities.

However, the following group of activities seemed to *fit* into "science" the best. So, when I arranged the activities into categories, "science" was the best description. The following group of activities are science "type" activities. They are not science experiments, per se, but they are science experiences. These activities will help your children begin to understand how colors mix together to make new colors; how magnets work and how elements react with one another (soap and water, oil and water etc.).

Best of all, these activities are fun, interesting, thought and conversation provoking. The ideas here are "*brain food.*" Your children will develop a few more brain cells and benefit infinitely more from these activities than if they watched their favorite video for the millionth time.

***Bigger-Ma-Jigger*:** **I'd better explain. According to Arial, *The Little Mermaid,* a magnifying glass is a "bigger-ma-jigger." I thought it was a cute way to describe a magnifying glass so I borrowed the term. Do you have a magnifying glass around the house? If so, your children will *love* to "inspect" things around the house. Children are natural born investigators. With a magnifying glass in hand, they may "discover" a whole new world right under their own feet.**

You can aid in expanding this experience by helping your children find things interesting to look at under a magnifying glass (buttons, earrings, food, leaves, the carpet, insects, each other's faces close up, etc.).

✂ Supplies You Will Need ✂

- ☆ **Magnifying glasses for each child. Of course plastic magnifying glasses would be the best but, most magnifying glasses have very thick glass and should not be prone to breakage. Close supervision is suggested though. This would be a good item to look for at your local thrift store.**

☺ Ways to Expand this Activity ☺

- ☆ **Here is an idea, for the scientist in the family. If insects don't bother you too much, try looking for a couple of earthworms or snails around the outside of your house. This may seem like a really yucky project but, your children will be fascinated by looking at these creatures under the magnifying glass. If you find earthworms or snails, scoop them up with a plastic spoon and put them onto a paper plate. Let your children observe how earthworms and snails move from point A to point B. Nature is amazing!**

Blowing Bubbles: This is one of my all-time personal favorites! It's cheap, easy and practically nothing to clean up. Best yet, your children will absolutely love this activity!

How many times have you told your children to stop blowing bubbles in their drink? Well here's their chance to blow bubbles galore. Give your children a plastic cup with about a 1/4 cup of water in it and a large squirt of liquid dishwasher detergent. I also suggest putting the cup into some kind of container, like a large Tupperware bucket/bowl, to catch the overflowing bubbles.

Now, let your children blow bubbles with a straw. They will squeal with delight!!! A word of caution, your children may not be used to <u>blowing</u> through the straw. Be sure to warn them that they will get a mouthful of soapy water if they suck on the straw. Therefore, I suggest you have your children blow a few "practice" blows into the water, just to be on the safe side, _before_ you add the liquid soap.

✄ _Supplies You Will Need_ ✄
☆ A clear plastic cup, so your children can see the bubbles coming out of the end of the straw.
☆ Liquid dishsoap. Dawn is the most bubbly, but it really doesn't matter what kind.

☺ _Ways to Expand this Activity_ ☺
FOR THE FOLLOWING VARIATIONS—PLEASE MAKE SURE YOUR CHILDREN REALLY KNOW HOW TO <u>BLOW</u> INTO THE WATER! YOU DON'T WANT THEM TO <u>DRINK</u> ANY OF THE FOLLOWING ITEMS:

☆ Add food coloring to the water to make colored bubbles.
☆ Add "fine" glitter to the water.
☆ Add Tempra paint to the water. Then, when your children have a good sized pile of bubbles, gently lay a piece of paper over top of the bubbles and make a bubble print.

Create a Magnet Box: **Children** *love* **magnets. All you need are a few magnets mixed in a box with several items both metal and non-metal. Your children can experiment with the items in the box to see what is magnetic. At your neighborhood pet store they sell "cow magnets." Farmers use cow magnets to collect metal pieces inside the stomachs of their livestock. The cow magnets are inexpensive and powerful. Children love them!**

✄ ***Supplies You Will Need*** ✄

☆ **Magnets, you can use the magnets off your refrigerator if you want or you can get magnets from the hardware or craft store. Magnets make great holiday or birthday gifts and/or the whole "magnet box" idea would be a terrific present idea.**

☺ ***Ways to Expand this Activity*** ☺

☆ **Throw in the ABC refrigerator magnets if your children have some.**

⌐A MOMMY TiP

Your neighborhood thrift store is a terrific resource! You can buy crazy hats, wigs, funny clothes for dress up. You can buy toys, electronic equipment and appliances for taking apart. Children <u>love</u> **to take things apart and what better than a** <u>real</u> **thing (toasters, clocks, cameras etc.) They have books and puzzles too!**
Makes a great "rainy day field trip" too!

Leaf Impressions: This may seem like a duplicate activity since it is basically the same thing as Object Rubbing in the Art section. I think this is different enough to be a separate activity though. This activity can open up a discussion between you and your children about how trees live. You might explain to your children how the veins carry water to the leaves. How trees breathe carbon dioxide and produce oxygen for <u>us</u> to breathe. This activity may start a big on-going discussion about our atmosphere, pollution and the environment. You just never really know what is going to happen when you expose your children to something new. That is why it is really important to give your children as many new experiences as possible. They are little sponges absorbing everything you put in front of them.

During a break in the rain, venture outside for a "field trip" to the backyard. Collect leaves of different shapes and sizes (it is best to use leaves that are still full of moisture inside). Then, place the leaves under a piece of not too thick paper. Remove the paper wrapper from a crayon and show your children how to press the crayon lengthwise across the paper. An image of the veins of the leaf will be transferred to the front side of the paper. Remember this from kindergarten? It's a classic!

<u>✄ _Supplies You Will Need_ ✄</u>
- ☆ Leaves of different shapes and sizes.
- ☆ Different thicknesses of paper.
- ☆ Crayons.

<u>☺ _Ways to Expand this Activity_ ☺</u>
- ☆ See if your children can cut the leaves out of the paper. If so, your children could make a fall/spring leaf wreath from the cut out leaves.

Magic Rainbow Celery: This activity may take a day to get results. But when you do, the results are really neat for children to see. This activity reinforces the Leaf Impression activity. It shows your children how plants "drink" water. Here is an opportunity to have a discussion with your children about how plants use water, sunlight, carbon monoxide and nutrients from the soil to produce their own food. That is *why* we have rain, to feed the plants. I think this activity is particularly appropriate on rainy days.

Here is what you do, split a stalk of celery from the bottom to about half way up the stalk. Make a fresh cut in the bottom of the stalk of celery to provide fresh holes for the celery to drink the water up through. Next, place each "leg" into a glass filled with food coloring and water. The next day you will see that the leaves of the celery stalk have absorbed the food coloring.

✄ *Supplies You Will Need* ✄
- ☆ A stalk of celery.
- ☆ Two different colors of food coloring.

☺ *Ways to Expand this Activity* ☺
- ☆ If you have a real fat stalk of celery you could split it into three sections.
- ☆ You can do this same trick with carnations too.
- ☆ Discuss pollution with your children. Explain what happens when the water, air and soil become contaminated with poisonous substances. If the soil and water become contaminated, plants will drink the contaminated water and will eventually die. If that happens, the plants will not be available to produce food and oxygen for humans and animals. Give a Hoot! Don't Pollute!

Mixing Colors: This is a fabulous activity! I did this activity with my preschool students at least once a week over my entire preschool teaching career. Amazingly, the children never got bored with it. Here's what you do. Fill an ice cube tray (white works best) with water and add different colors of food coloring to each compartment. With an eye dropper, your children can experiment by mixing the different colors together. This activity may be best for children who are a little older (3-5 yrs. old). It takes some skill to use an eye dropper, but even a younger child can master it with help and practice.

✂ _**Supplies You Will Need**_ ✂
- ☆ A white ice cube tray.
- ☆ Food coloring.
- ☆ Eye droppers.

☺ _**Ways to Expand this Activity**_ ☺
- ☆ Suction cup soap holders are a great addition to this activity. Your children can use the suction cups to collect "drops" of colored water. This activity takes practice and concentration and can keep your children busy for a long time!
  This activity was one of my old standbys as a preschool teacher.
- ☆ Put glitter into the colored water.
- ☆ Freeze the colored ice cubes then let your children play with the ice cubes in a tub of water.
- ☆ Add a small drop of liquid dishsoap into each compartment and give your children a straw to blow bubbles with.

Rainbow Water: This activity will be very interesting for your children. You will need a glass jar for this activity. Plastic will not work because you need to be able to see through the side of the container. Fill the glass jar, the larger and taller the better, about 3/4 of the way with water. Then, add a small amount of cooking oil. Of course, they will separate and the oil will float on top of the water. Then, let your children add single drops of food coloring into the oil. The resulting effect is really neat. The food coloring will slowly sink through the oil making an interesting design as it goes. Then, when the food coloring reaches the water, it makes a rainbow effect.

✂ _**Supplies You Will Need**_ ✂
- ☆ A large glass jar. A one-gallon pickle jar is perfect, but a tall vase will work well too.
- ☆ Water.
- ☆ About a half a cup of cooking oil.
- ☆ Food coloring.

☺ _**Ways to Expand this Activity**_ ☺
- ☆ None.

⌂ MOMMY TiP

When your children begin to develop their imagination, monsters will probably become an issue in your house. One way of giving the _power_ back to your children over monsters is to make up a special batch of "Monster Repellent" (water, food coloring and fragrant food flavoring in a spray bottle.) Whenever there is a "monster" in the house just give'em a squirt. Presto, monsters gone! I just used an old hairspray bottle. Your children will love it and it works great. I hardly ever hear _anything_ about monsters anymore.

Vinegar & Baking Soda: Remember your fourth grade volcano experiment? The one where you built a volcano from chicken wire and papier-mâché. Once you had built the volcano, you poured vinegar down into the cavity inside the volcano, THEN, with great anticipation, you put a tablespoon or two of baking soda into the vinegar. Instant eruption!

Imagine how thrilled your preschooler will be when they get to play with such a reactive combination. This is a really neat activity for young children. As long as they don't try to eat or drink it they'll have a blast. It won't hurt them but, they may be unhappy with how it tastes.

Set your children up using a big tray (for run over) and a couple of small containers. I have found that a tall see through container like a plastic cigar tube works well to pour the vinegar into because your children will be able to see inside where the chemical reaction is happening.

Put baking soda in one container (a small bowl is fine) and vinegar in the tall see through container. Let your children spoon baking soda into the vinegar. Use the smallest spoon you have. After a few of scoops of baking soda the vinegar will begin to lose it's fizz. Just add new vinegar.

✃ *Supplies You Will Need* ✃
- ☆ Fresh vinegar. For some odd reason this seems to work better with new from the store vinegar.
- ☆ Baking soda.
- ☆ Small (narrow) tall see through container for the vinegar. A tall, small jelly jar will work too.

☺ *Ways to Expand this Activity* ☺
- ☆ After your children have gotten to see what this does, add some food coloring.
- ☆ Dissolve some baking soda in water (make sure it is very concentrated), then add the baking soda water to the vinegar. What a kick!
- ☆ Add one color of food coloring to the vinegar and a different color food coloring to the water/baking soda solution then mix them together. They will bubble into a new color. Neat!

Waterplay: Water is an excellent _toy!_ There is just something mesmerizing and soothing about water. Children just love to play with it! The water table is always one of the favorite spots in the preschool classrooms. Now you can have you own water table at home. Your children will love it!

Fill a shallow tub (you can use the same one that you used for the beans, cornmeal or rice) with warm water and kitchen utensils. Let your children experiment with measuring, pouring and blowing bubbles (with a straw). To make it real easy on yourself just fill up your sink about half way with warm water and let your children go to town. This activity may require close supervision and you might want to cover your children with a smock.

✄ _Supplies You Will Need_ ✄

☆ A large tray of some kind. See page 91 under "supplies you will need."

☆ Measuring cups, funnels, strainers, different kinds of spoons (measuring, wooden, plastic), eye droppers and whatever other odd utensils you have laying around.

☺ _Ways to Expand this Activity_ ☺

☆ Add food coloring to the water.

☆ Add colored ice cubes to the water.

☆ Add a little dish soap for bubbles.

☆ Let your children have an egg beater (hand operated) to use in the water to make bubbles.

☆ Add all of the above all at once.

☆ Let your children wash a baby doll or some of their toys.

☆ At your local teacher's supply store you will find all sorts of special waterplay toys. They have water wheels and hand-held pumps and strainers and special funnels with tubes attached, lots of great things for waterplay.

☆ Save empty glue bottles to let your children use in the water. They make good squirters.

☆ Save empty plastic lotion bottles with the pump top for waterplay.

Sugar-Free Stocking Stuffer Ideas...

The following list can also be used for Easter Baskets, Halloween treats,
Valentine's Day goodies etc. to replace sugary items.

3 Minute Timer
Adding Machine Tape
Balsa Wood
Bingo Stamp Paints
Box of Bandaids
Bubbles
Chalk
Chap Stick
Children's Scissors
Cookie Cutters
Crayons
Deck of Cards
Disposable Camera
Duct Tape
Elmer's Glue
Felt Pens
Felt Squares

Flashlight
Golf Tees
Hole Punch
Index Cards
Jello
Jiffy Pop
Little Books
Magnets
Magnifying Glass
Marbles
Molding Clay
Movie Tickets or a Video
New Box of Envelopes
Novelty Ice Cube Trays
Padlock & Key
Paint Brushes
Paper Note Pads

Pipe cleaners
Plastic Tapestry Needles
Playdough Toys
Play Money/Poker Chips
Popsicle Molds
Real Stethoscope
Real Tools
Scotch Tape
Shaving Cream
Sponges in Shapes
Stamps & Stamp Pad
Stickers
Sticky Dots
Tracing Templates
Turkey Baster
Watercolor paints
Wigs

SENSORY ACTIVITIES

Mud Pies—*but no mud involved?*

This next group of activities are akin to "playing with mud pies" but not as dirty, maybe just as *messy,* but no dirt is involved. Phew! This group of activities is also very likely to be your children's all-time favorites. As you read through the following group of activities, just keep reminding yourself that all messes can be cleaned and that you are providing your children with wonderful childhood memories to fondly look back on as they recall their youth. They are only going to be children once!

Be sure to have a bucket of water nearby for hand washing. You wouldn't want to try to get your children down the hall and into the bathroom, with their messy hands and who knows what else. Oh, remember to get out your camera!

Finger painting with Pudding: Sounds fun doesn't it? Your children will love this activity, especially if they like to play with their food and you are always telling them to stop. Give your children a tray (hostess or cookie sheet) and plop a big scoop of pudding on it. Of course, have them wash their hands really well before starting this. Then, let them go to town. Before long they may be covered in the stuff, but oh what fun it is!

✳ *Supplies You Will Need* ✳

☆ Your children's favorite flavor of instant pudding. Make it easy on yourself, use ready-made pudding in the cups. My son prefers freshly made noninstant though, because it isn't as cold as ready-made pudding that comes out of the refrigerator. You will have to test your children to see what goes over better with them.

☆ A tray of some kind.

☆ Definitely a smock!

☺ *Ways to Expand this Activity* ☺

☆ You might add sprinkles to the pudding to give it some texture.

☆ You could start with two different flavors/colors of pudding and let your children mix them together.

☆ This may be a way to teach your children about colors. Make vanilla pudding, dividing the batch in half and add different colors of food coloring to each half. For example, make half the batch red and half blue. Then, when your children mix them together, they will make purple. This could be a seasonal activity, red and white for Valentines Day; green for St. Patrick's Day; red, white and blue for Fourth of July etc.

☆ After the novelty wears off, throw in a few apple chunks or banana slices or marshmallows to further the experience and fun. This would be extra tasty with chocolate pudding, but any flavor pudding will do just fine.

Finger painting with Shaving Cream: This is a great activity! This is probably one of the most frequent activities in preschool classrooms because children love it and it is relatively easy to clean up. It is also very good for sensory and brain development. Your children will _love_ it! Fortunately it is a lot cleaner than regular finger painting (although your children may get carried away so supervision is still necessary). If you have a table that needs a good cleaning, this activity can kill two birds with one stone. Shaving cream is soap so it cleans whatever surface you put it on. If you would rather not "dirty" up a table, then you can use a tray of some sort (hostess tray, cookie sheet etc.). If you do decide to use a table top, the quick and easy way to clean up is to use a window squeegee to scrape off the shaving cream.

✂ _Supplies You Will Need_ ✂
- ☆ A couple of cans of shaving cream. You can usually buy an off brand for about a dollar a can.
- ☆ Hostess tray or cookie sheet.
- ☆ Smocks!

☺ _Ways to Expand this Activity_ ☺
- ☆ Add glitter.
- ☆ Add food coloring.
- ☆ Add paint.
- ☆ Add something of texture like rice or beans to change the feel of it.
- ☆ Or spice things up a bit by buying a can of scented shaving cream.
- ☆ Instead of buying a can of scented shaving cream add your own scent (perfume, cologne, peppermint or other food flavoring/scent).

Finger painting with Whipped Cream: Imagine how fun this is! On a tray, give your children a glob of whipped cream. Get ready for the giggles, you and your children are bound to have quite a few.

✂ *Supplies You Will Need* ✂
- ☆ A couple of cans of whipping cream.
- ☆ A smock.

☺ *Ways to Expand this Activity* ☺
- ☆ You can also add food coloring to the whipped cream and/or marshmallows, sprinkles, nuts.

Goop: This is simple. In a 9" x 13" baking dish, combine cornstarch and water. First add the cornstarch. Then, slowly add in about half as much water as you have cornstarch. At first the cornstarch will be very thick and gooey. Slowly add more water until the goop becomes manageable. Then, let your children dig in. Cornstarch and water has a *very* interesting texture. It feels wet and dry at the same time. Your children will be intrigued for a long time. You probably could do this once a week until your children are teenagers and they would never get bored with it. This activity is easy to clean up too. If it gets on clothes or the carpet, just let it dry and it will vacuum right up.

✂ *Supplies You Will Need* ✂
- ☆ A box of cornstarch.
- ☆ Water.
- ☆ Lots of kitchen utensils and gadgets.

☺ *Ways to Expand this Activity* ☺
- ☆ Add food coloring or Kool-Aid.
- ☆ Add glitter.
- ☆ Add rice or confetti.

Homemade Silly Putty: This activity is one of the most interesting of all the activities offered in this book. _You_ and your children will enjoy playing with this concoction. It is similar to playdough yet very different at the same time. It is hard to describe, but it is fascinating to play with. It behaves like stretchy, rubbery dough and it's very shiny. If pulled apart it "breaks" sharply as if you have cut it, then molds back together when you knead it. It's enchanting stuff!

To make silly putty (it is also called Gak) dissolve ¼ c. Borax in a quart of water. Next, in a different container (with a lid) combined 1 c. of Elmer's glue with 1 c. of water (shake well). In a third container combine 2 Tbsp. Borax solution with 6 Tbsp. glue solution. Make more as needed.

As you add the glue solution you will notice the mixture chemically reacting. It instantly turns from a liquid to a semi-solid compound. Stir to mix everything together and pour off excess liquid. Next turn onto a paper plate and knead it a bit until it is no longer sticky (it firms up right away). Now for the best part, give it to your children. They will be enthralled! If you never do any other activity suggested in this book, do this one! One final note—don't let this get on your carpet.

✀ _Supplies You Will Need_ ✀
- ☆ 1 Quart of water.
- ☆ ¼ cup Borax* (available in the laundry section of your grocery store). **Supervision Required!**
- ☆ 1 cup of Elmer's glue.
- ☆ 1 cup of water.
- ☆ Containers (one with a lid). Save your solutions for another day. Any 3 to 1 ratio will work.

☺ _Ways to Expand this Activity_ ☺
- ☆ Add a little food coloring to the glue before mixing it with the Borax.
- ☆ With a straw, bubbles can be blown from the silly putty. Put a straw under a blob and blow.
- ☆ Let your children draw on it with watercolor markers then knead it and pull it apart.

* Supervise your children with this activity. The Borax in the mix may be harmful if swallowed.

Sandcastles: Do you have a sandbox in your backyard? Even if you don't, maybe your neighbor does and would let you borrow a couple of buckets of sand for a few days. Set your children up with a tray (again, the plastic under the bed box is fine) and fill it with sand. Add a couple of cups or so of water to make it moist, then pretend you are all at the beach. This may be even better than the beach because your children will have access to *all* of your kitchen utensils. They may be able to make an even neater sandcastle than they would have been able to do at the beach. You could really expand the "beach" theme and let your children get dressed up in their bathing suits. After they are done with their sandcastles, have a beach style picnic in the living room.

If your children are not really into making sandcastles (or they are just too little), you can just let them make roads and play in the sand with a toy truck and little people.

✂ *Supplies You Will Need* ✂
- ☆ A large tray of some kind. See page 91 under "supplies you will need."
- ☆ Sand.
- ☆ Sand toys.

☺ *Ways to Expand this Activity* ☺
- ☆ After your children have gotten tired of just plain sand add a little (just a little) dry tempra paint to the sand and presto—colored sand.
- ☆ Bathtub toys make good sand toys.
- ☆ You can throw in a toilet paper tube or two or you might have an interesting container or two that is supposed to go into recycling that your children could use for the time being.
- ☆ Just for fun, throw in a few pennies or other coins when your children are not looking. See what happens when they find the coins. They will be so excited!
- ☆ Marbles would be a fun addition too.

Scented Playdough (Homemade): The recipe included here is the best playdough recipe I have found. It's quick and easy to make and it lasts a long, long time with proper care. When your children are finished playing with it, wrap it up in a one gallon food storage bag and put it into a Tupperware® bowl with a tight lid. At the school, playdough never lasted very long. The children just love it and play with it all of the time. However, at home, I have had it last for almost a year without it getting too dried out. Recently, I have discovered that when playdough becomes dried out you can revive it. Slightly wet your hands and knead it for a little while, even playdough that is crusty on the edges will moisten right up.

Another great thing about this playdough recipe is that it will not stain clothing or carpeting. If it gets into clothing (which is rarely a problem) just let it soak for a while before running it through the washing machine. It will come right out. If it gets into the carpet, and it gets ground in, just let it dry and it will flake right out without leaving any marks.

When you make this playdough you will find that is is very fragrant. The Kool-aid in the recipe acts as a coloring *and* a fragrance. Your children will love playing with playdough that smells like grape or cherry plus the added scent extends the playdough experience quite a bit. Playdough is a lot of fun when it has little or no smell, but added scent brings the experience to a whole new level.

A few words on playdough . . . playdough is a **GREAT** toy! Children love it and it is very, very good for their development. Playdough single handedly handles lots and lots of development issues. It is a sensory experience. It helps develop hand-eye coordination. It encourages your children to use their imagination. And best yet, because playdough helps develop all of those other areas, it is also good for their self-esteem. Let your children play with it often (everyday if they want). They will be better people for it. They will be better students in school and have higher self-esteem.

✂ *Supplies You Will Need* ✂

2 c. flour
1/2 c. salt
2 packages Kool-Aid (unsweetened)
2 T. vegetable oil
1 1/4 c. hot water separated. Reserve 1/4 c. of the water and add very slowly as needed.

First mix the flour, salt and Kool-Aid together. Stir well prior to adding the water and oil. Here is your opportunity to *wow* your children. The dry Kool-aid has very little color. However, when you add in the hot water the Kool-aid bursts into its' respective color. For a young child it looks like magic because the flour mixture is basically white and the water is clear yet when you pour the water in it instantly turns a vibrant color. It's neat. After adding in the water and oil stir with a large spoon until it sticks together fairly well. Slowly add the remaining 1/4 c. of water a little at a time. When it has formed into a ball sufficiently so that you can pick it up, move it to a bread board. Generously "dust" your bread board with flour, knead additional flour into the playdough until it becomes the right consistency. You will be able to fine tune it the more often you make it.

☺ *Ways to Expand this Activity* ☺

☆ I have a large basket filled with all sorts of regular kitchen gadgets as well as unusual kitchen gadgets for my son to use while he is playing with his playdough. I always use birthdays, Christmas and Easter etc. as opportunities to expand his playdough "tools." I usually buy a new set of cookie cutters, some umbrella toothpicks or play utensils (knives, forks, spoons, plates and cups etc.) to add to his collection. I don't really like the playdough toys that are available in toy stores. I feel they are too limiting. "Real" tools are more interesting.

☆ Playdough is very, very versatile. You can add all sorts of things to it to make it more interesting; glitter: rice, confetti, etc.

Shaving with Shaving Cream: No not _real_ shaving, just pretend. Give your children a popsicle stick, a handful of shaving cream and a mirror. I have found that putting the shaving cream on a paper plate or in a plastic bowl works well. Your children can help themselves to more shaving cream when they want it, but they will not have access to the whole can. Phew! Let them apply the shaving cream to their face and pretend to shave like Daddy/Grandpa does. You may want to plan to throw them in the tub after they "shave." Often, the shaving cream ends up in the hair and all over their clothes. No need to worry about stained clothes here though, shaving cream is soap and will easily come out of your children's clothes in the wash. Instruct your children to be careful of their eyes. Of course, be sure to have film in the camera or the vidoe camera battery charged!

✄ _Supplies You Will Need_ ✄
- ☆ Shaving cream.
- ☆ Popsicle sticks.
- ☆ Mirror.
- ☆ Smocks!

☺ _Ways to Expand this Activity_ ☺
- ☆ If you have a shaving brush around, let your children use it to apply the shaving cream.
- ☆ Let your children "shave" right in the tub. If you have a small unbreakable makeup mirror that will stand up by itself on the side of the tub, let your children use it to pretend to shave.
- ☆ Blow up a balloon and let your children try to "shave" the balloon with a popsicle stick.
- ☆ If your children are not to sure about putting shaving cream on their face, because their face is too sensitve, let them shave their arms, tummy or legs instead. The skin on the face is very sensitive and it is not all that uncommon for young children to be protective of their face. As children get older they become less concerned and are more willing to try new things.

TABLE TOP ACTIVITIES

This group of activities is for your children, once they have gotten all their wiggles out and are ready for quieter things to do. Most of these activities involve paper, tape, crayons, felt pens, scissors, basically "clean" art supplies. Not much gooey stuff to clean up here!☺ These activities are simple, clean and child friendly (meaning that your children will be able to do most of these activities on their own or with minimal supervision). They are great for helping children develop hand-eye coordination and small motor skills.

You and your children are probably already familiar with most of these activities and have done them many times in the past. But, I threw them in anyway because, on a rainy day, there is a lot of time to kill and even those ideas that are familiar may escape your memory banks at the time when you need them most. It is so hard to think under pressure!

I know from my own experience, even though I have hundreds of ideas for activities in my head, right at the moment when I really need *SOMETHING* for my students or my son to do, *RIGHT NOW*, I draw a total blank and can't think of one single thing beyond crayons and paper or playdough. At times like these, I would give anything for a good list of even old familiar activities that are relative clean and easy to set up just to get me through the next hour. So, even though these ideas are not all that exciting and new, they are still fun and will chase boredom away! *ENJOY!*

Adding Machine Tape: This activity is probably better suited for children who are a little older say 4 1/2 to 5 and on up. Give your children a roll of adding machine tape or two and see what happens. They may come up with all kinds of terrific ideas or they may just want to color on it. Other things that they can do (you may have to make a few suggestions) is to make headbands, wristbands and anklebands. Then, color them with crayons, felt pens or watercolor paints.

✂ **_Supplies You Will Need_** ✂
- ☆ Adding machine tape.
- ☆ A stapler. Be sure to staple with the opening to the outside so that the staples do not scratch your child.
- ☆ Use tape instead of a stapler.
- ☆ Crayons, felt pens and/or watercolor paints.

☺ **_Ways to Expand this Activity_** ☺
- ☆ A roll of adding machine tape makes a fun stocking stuffer.
- ☆ Stamps are extra fun on adding machine tape.
- ☆ Stickers added to the headbands and wristband could make quite a stylish statement.
- ☆ Add bunny ears in the front and a couple of cotton balls to the back of a headband and presto—bunnies!
- ☆ Add streamers for fun. The list goes on and on, the possibilities are endless!

Clothespins: Here's a no brainer. Give your children a shoe box or a wicker basket to put clothes-pins on (around the rim). This activity seems so simple, but children really like it for some reason and there is no mess to clean up. It works out nicely if the number of clothespins "fits" exactly around the rim of the box or basket. This is a good hand-eye coordination skill builder.

✀ *Supplies You Will Need* ✀
- ☆ Clothespins.
- ☆ Something to clip the clothespins onto, a small cardboard box or basket.

☺ *Ways to Expand this Activity* ☺
- ☆ If you are not too particular about how your clothespins look, you could give your children some felt pens and let them color on them.

MOMMY TIP

Save the color store ads that come in the mail or your newspaper for your children to use to cut up. Use the pictures in a collage or as a way to tell a story.

Magazine Art: Here is a good use for all of those old magazines. This requires scissors, so supervision is recommended. You can either give your children a couple of old magazines and let them cut away or you can give them "instructions." For example, look for babies, cars, fire engines, food, bicycles, birthday presents etc. or whatever else you and your children can think of. Then, have your children collect their "cutouts" and glue them to a piece of paper. This can be a good activity for children who are a little older and are starting to learn the alphabet. You can help your children find letters to their name, your name, Daddy's name, their favorite playmate's name, you get the idea. You can also look for numbers, (this would be a good way to teach your children their phone number, street address and how to call 911) colors, shapes and/or anything else "academic" that you want them to learn. Not only is this activity great for teaching your children letters, numbers, shapes etc. but, it also helps to develop "cutting with scissors skills."

✂ *Supplies You Will Need* ✂
- ☆ Magazines.
- ☆ Tape or glue (glue sticks would come in handy here).
- ☆ Paper to glue their pictures on.
- ☆ Children's scissors.

☺ *Ways to Expand this Activity* ☺
- ☆ Your children can make their own matching game by finding matching pictures and gluing or taping the pictures onto 3" x 5" cards.
- ☆ If you do not have any old magazines around, pictures in your junk mail may do. Neighbors or relatives may be willing to part with a few old magazines. You may also find magazines in thrift shops.
- ☆ The newspaper is another resource for finding letters, numbers and shapes to cut out.

Memory: If you have an old deck of cards laying around, put it to good use. Set up a game of memory. The object of memory is to collect the most sets of matching cards. Don't worry about the "suit" of the card. Pick through the deck and choose matching numbers. You do not have to use the whole deck. Lay the cards out face down and everyone gets a chance to turn two cards over. If the cards match, then that person gets to keep that matching set of cards. When the cards are all matched up, the person with the most matches wins. This is a really good rainy day activity. Children really enjoy playing this and they are willing to stay at it for quite a while.

✄ _Supplies You Will Need_ ✄

- ☆ A deck of cards.
- ☆ They also sell matching games in toy stores. If your children really love this game it would be a good investment to purchase one, maybe for a birthday gift.

☺ _Ways to Expand this Activity_ ☺

- ☆ You can make your own memory game by making "matching" 3" x 5" cards. Draw shapes, numbers, letters, or use matching stickers on 3" x 5" cards.
- ☆ Make a memory game from left over juice can lids (finally a use for those lids). Collect juice can lids until you have a dozen or more. Put matching stickers* on one side and leave the other side blank. Put the juice can lids out on a table upside down and let the matching begin!
- ☆ Once your children get really good at this game, see if they can match three items. Tricky!

* Using ordinary stickers or adhesive letters, numbers, shapes, colors, textures, scratch & sniff stickers, cut large stickers in half and match the halves, match dots (put 1,2,3,4 etc. dots on one side of the juice cans lid and make a matching lid for each number of dots and match the dots). Lots of possibilities here!

Paper Bag Apparel: If you make a habit of asking for plastic bags at the supermarket, then the next few times you go shopping, ask for paper bags. They make great masks, vests, suits of armor, and just all around good play items. Children can find lots of things to make out of them. If your children are "into" something lately (super heroes, insects, princesses etc.), here is a way to play on their on-going theme. Help them make the special vest, suit of armor, crown or whatever it is that is special about their favorite activity right now.

✂ Supplies You Will Need ✂
- ☆ Paper grocery bags.
- ☆ Crayons, felt pens or if you are really daring—paint.
- ☆ Scraps of fabric.

☺ Ways to Expand this Activity ☺
- ☆ Accessorize with aluminum foil props (crowns, swords, wristbands, diamonds, etc.).

⌂ MOMMY TiP

For all you Moms who have an only child, here's a tip. There is practically no better day to invite your child's friends over for a visit, than on a rainy day. Nothing chases boredom away faster than companionship, plus your child and their guest(s) will really have an entertaining time if they get to do a few of the activities in this book!

Paper Chains: Here is a super easy activity! This activity may be a good one for keeping your children busy for short periods of time, say in-between errands, when you don't want your children to make a big mess but, you want them to be doing something constructive.

This is also a good "finish it later" activity. If you have other things on your agenda for the day, you can set your children up with this activity. Then, stop them whenever you need to because they can stop without having to clean anything up. Your children can easily pick it up again when you all return home.

Some other good points about this activity are that you can use *any* kind of paper. There is very little mess to contend with, and your children can make paper chains anytime without much supervision from you (once they know how to make them).

I'm certain everyone reading this book has at some point in their life made paper chains, but just to be on the safe side, here is what you do.

Cut paper into strips about 1 or 2 inches wide by 8 inches long. Older children can help with this. If you have a pretty young child who has good cutting skills you can help build on those skills by giving them a piece of paper with lines drawn across and let them help cut out the strips too. Once you have lots of strips cut out then loop one paper strip around into a circle and fasten the ends together. You/your children can use tape or a stapler to fasten the ends together. (You may be concerned about letting your very small children use a stapler, but with proper instructions children as young as three can correctly use a stapler without injury. Close supervision is required).

After the first loop is made, keep looping the strips of paper together and fastening the ends. Before long, your children will have a chain of paper.

✂ *Supplies You Will Need* ✂

☆ Any kind of paper will do. Save flyers that you receive in the mail for cutting up, that way you will have different colors to pick from. Construction paper makes sturdy paper chains and you have a better choice of colors, but you can't beat the price of flyers that come free in the mail.

☆ Tape or a stapler.

☆ Crayons or felt pens for coloring on the paper before cutting it up into strips.

☆ Scissors. As your children get older they will be learning how to use scissors themselves, and after a while they will be able to cut the strips of paper on their own.

☺ *Ways to Expand this Activity* ☺

☆ Let your children stamp with stamp pads and make ink stamps on the strips of paper before looping and fasten them.

☆ Help your children begin to learn their colors by making a sample chain for them and have them try to copy the sequence of the colors. This is a skill that is worked on quite a bit in kindergarten, patterning that is. Your children's future kindergarten teacher will thank you for teaching your children how to see and copy patterns.

☆ Have your children make paper chains to decorate a room for an up coming birthday party or special event.

☆ Make paper chains to decorate for an up coming holiday (white, pink and red for Valentine's Day, green and white for St. Patrick's Day, pastels for Easter, etc.).

☆ Challenge your children to make a paper chain the length of your house. Children love challenges like these. (The problem is what to do with a chain the length of you house?)

Paper Plates: You can do a lot with paper plates. Here are a few ideas:

Coloring paper plates: Simple dimple! Children can get really creative when coloring on paper plates. They can come up with all sorts of things to make out of them. Color with crayons, felt pens, chalk, stamps, stickers, watercolors, glue & glitter.

Hats: Cut out the middle and let your children decorate and wear the rim for a hat. Add streamers and/or a tail (dinosaur, bunny, cat, fish, lizard, tails, etc.).

Mail boxes: Cut one paper plate in half and "sew" (with yarn), staple, tape or glue the half paper plate to a whole paper plate (face to face, which forms a pocket) and there you have a mail box for your children to receive mail. This mail box idea can be used when your children play "office."

Masks: Cut holes for eyes, nose and mouth then let your children decorate with crayons, felt pens, paint, etc. yarn or cotton for hair. Tie string to each side of the paper plate then tie in the back to hold onto the children's face.

Sewing: Punch holes around the edge of the paper plate and give your children some yarn to "sew" through the holes. You can either wrap tape around one end of the yarn (to prevent fraying) or let your children use a plastic needle.

Stencils: Paper plates make great stencils. You don't have to be the least bit talented to make stencils. Cut out circles, squares, triangles, birds, animals, flowers, letters, numbers, dinosaurs whatever you can think of and let your children trace inside the cut out part. Use puzzle pieces for patterns. These stencils will keep for a while too so you can use them over and over.

Tambourines: Fold a paper plate in half and put beans, elbow macaroni, buttons etc. inside and sew or staple the edges together. Add a couple of streamers for flare.

Stacking Cheerios: Cheerios were a great invention! Place a piece of dry spaghetti into a glob of playdough (standing straight up). Let your children "thread or stack" the Cheerios onto the piece of spaghetti. This activity has a lot of variations. You can let your children stack Fruit Loops, colored macaroni, buttons, a straw cut into short pieces etc.

✄ **_Supplies You Will Need_** ✄
- ☆ Cheerios.
- ☆ Spaghetti.
- ☆ Playdough or molding clay.

☺ **_Ways to Expand this Activity_** ☺
- ☆ Break the spaghetti into two or more shorter pieces and let each child have a few Cheerio stacks.
- ☆ Use pipecleaners instead of spaghetti.
- ☆ After your children have finished stacking the Cheerios, gently attach a piece of string/yarn to the top of the spaghetti and flip it over. Presto! Your children have a Cheerio necklace. Cheerio necklaces are great toys for children in the grocery store. For once they are focused on something besides climbing in and out of the cart and/or pulling things off the shelves.

Stamps and Stamp Pads: Here is another all-time favorite! You can buy stamps all over the place now. It is quite a popular activity. If you don't want to go to the expense of buying "special" stamps, just let your children use whatever stamps you have in your desk. If you don't have any stamps or only have a couple, you can make stamps from bicycle innertubes or foot padding innersoles (just peel off backing and stick onto wood blocks).

After you have cut out shapes (they don't have to be fancy) glue the shapes onto blocks of wood. Your children will have just as much fun with stamps that cost pennies as they would with stamps that cost $2 or $3 dollars each. Making your own stamps may seem like a lot of work, but this is an activity that you can do *with* your children. Once you have made them, your children will have them to play with forever.

✂ *Supplies You Will Need* ✂

☆ Nontoxic, watercolor stamp pads. Stamp pads make great stocking stuffers!

☆ Superglue® for gluing the shapes onto the blocks of wood.

☆ Stamps and/or materials to make stamps.

☆ Paper.

☺ *Ways to Expand this Activity* ☺

☆ Another way to make stamps is out of sponges sliced thin and glued on to blocks of wood.

☆ Make a set of alphabet and/or number stamps. You can buy stencils or templets of letters and numbers at the craft or stationery store if you would like for your letters/numbers to look more "professional." Tupperware® has large sets of tracing templets with small letters, numbers, animals, shapes etc. that would make beautiful stamps. Just trace the shapes onto your stamp material, cut out and glue onto blocks of wood. Presto, cheap stamps!

"Tee" Time: Don't panic! I'm not suggesting golf in the house. This is an idea for a matching game. This will require a little "handiwork" on your part. What you will need to do is make a "matching board" for your children to match colored golf tees to their respective color.

Cardboard will probably work the best. Using a small gift box (one with a sturdy lid), quarter the top by drawing an X on the top of the box. You should have a box with four squares on top. Color in the different sections with felt pen (watercolor paint or crayon). Then, punch golf tee size holes, either randomly or in a pattern, in the top of the box.

The object of this activity is for your children to "match" colored golf tees to the appropriate "color" on the box lid. For some reason this activity really holds children's attention. A teacher that I worked with made one of these golf tee boxes for the children at the school. It seems like a silly little toy that children would play with a couple of times and then not be interested in it anymore. But, for some reason, this was one of the favorite toys at the school. The children played and played with it for about a year until it finally fell apart. That is why I included it in this book, because I know children really enjoy this game.

✂ _Supplies You Will Need_ ✂
☆ A board made from a box or a ceiling tile with holes in it will also work.

☆ Colored golf tees. You can also buy white golf tees and paint them yourself with spray paint.

☺ _Ways to Expand this Activity_ ☺
☆ If you want to get really fancy and/or you have a handy husband at home, then you can make your "matching board" from wood by drilling holes in a flat board. Then, color or paint the squares to match the golf tees.

Tracing: Tracing things is very good for developing your children's hand-eye coordination and developing the muscles in their hands. This is only limited by your imagination. Let your children trace around puzzle pieces, Tupperware® lids, tuna cans, blocks etc. Then, to extend the activity, let your children cut out their tracing (with supervision of course).

✂ **_Supplies You Will Need_** ✂
- ☆ Things to trace.
- ☆ Paper.
- ☆ Scissors.
- ☆ Crayons, felt pens, colored pencils.

☺ **_Ways to Expand this Activity_** ☺
- ☆ You can buy "children's" templates at your local teacher's supply store. Children's templets have big letters and numbers for tracing. Templets make great stocking stuffers.
- ☆ Children love to use templets. At your local office supply store you can also buy templets that professional draftsmen use. The letters, numbers and shapes are small so the professional templets may be better for children who are a little older and have better developed writing skills.

Write to the Relatives: What better time than a rainy day to catch up on past due letters to far away relatives. Have your children each draw pictures or make hand and foot print paintings to send. The easiest and least messy way to make hand and foot print paintings is to use a paint-brush and paint your children's hands with paint. Next, help your children press their hands carefully onto a piece of paper. Do the same thing with their feet. Your children will love it! The recipient will love it too!

Another idea would be for each one of your children to make up a special book about themselves. They can draw pictures of their favorite things, then dictate to you what their pictures are about. You might write their stories on the back of their pictures.

This might be a good project to start in preparation of an upcoming holiday or birthday. Any far off relative would be tickled pink to receive a package that so much attention and effort went into.

✂ _Supplies You Will Need_ ✂
- ☆ Lots of stationery supplies. Paper, felt pens, crayons, envelopes, stickers, etc.
- ☆ Postage stamps. Maybe in honor of this special package buy special "love" stamps.
- ☆ A large envelope or box to hold all the special goodies.

☺ _Ways to Expand this Activity_ ☺
- ☆ Bake cookies to send along with all the special pictures and stories.
- ☆ Take pictures of your children drawing their pictures or making their hand/foot print paintings and send the photo pictures along too.
- ☆ Do you have a tape recorder? Tape record your children singing, talking, laughing and send along an audio tape. How precious!
- ☆ Better yet, instead of just pictures, send a video made just for this mailing.

Additional Resources . . .

Trying to figure out what to do with your children to entertain them is an on-going quest for every parent. Listed below are some other high caliber activity books filled with fun *quality* things to do with young children. Also, see the children's craft section at your local library and at your local bookstore. There are dozen and dozens of activity and cooking books for children, covering every topic imaginable.

Rainy Day Activities for Preschoolers: Ann Marie Connolly and Helen Gibson, Mercer Island Preschool Association, 1988. Available through your local library or Amazon.com
   Lots of great ideas and recipes for homemade fingerpaint and clay playdough for preschoolers. Of all the books I checked out from the library during my research, this book was one of the best. I highly recommend it!

Klutz Press Books: Klutz Press has a mail order catalogue that is filled with a couple dozen or so books on things to do with children and things for older children to learn—like *How to do Magic Tricks, Face Painting Ideas, Juggling, Kids Cooking,* etc. You can get a copy of the Klutz catalogue by calling (415)857-0888.

Discount School Supply Catalogue-Easier than a Store: Discount School Supply 1(800)627-2829 or on the Web at www.earlychildhood.com. This catalogue is *filled* with marvelous art supplies, toys, games, children's furniture, educational materials etc. This company is where many child care centers buy their supplies to stock their school classrooms. There are many, many such school supplies companies out there, but Discount School Supply has some of the very best prices available. You could do all your holiday shopping for your children, from your kitchen table and get some of the best prices in town using this catalogue! Best of all, the catalogue is FREE, just call and ask for a copy. They ship nationwide. Before adding this information I called and asked Discount School Supply if it was OK for me to make this information available. They gave me the go ahead, YEAH, so tell your friends about Discount School Supply too, they are a terrific resource for parents.

The Mudpies Activity Book—Recipes for Invention: Nancy Blakey, Tricycle Press P.O. Box 7123 Berkeley, California 94707. 1-800-841-BOOK.
   This is one of the standby, preschool teacher's, resource book. You can find this book in almost every preschool around the country. It's filled with original creative ideas. You can order a catalogue from Tricycle Press by calling the number listed and leaving your name and address on their answering machine. They have several other books to choose from so their catalogue is a good resource for parents.

Your local child care referral service will have current listings of the child care conferences and other child care events in your area. You may attend these events even if you are not working in the child care industry. Ask to be added to their mailing list to receive conference information.

The Tools of the Trade

Now that you have all these great ideas for keeping your children busy, happy and entertained during those long rainy days, you will need "supplies" to put together the projects for your children. The following is a complete list of _ALL_ the supplies, ingredients, tools, props, and equipment etc. that you will need to complete _ANY_ of the projects in this book.

This list was compiled and put at the back of the book so that it would be easy to make copies of. The next time you go to the grocery store, hardware store, or craft store (with list in hand), you can begin collecting the supplies you need. That way when those long rainy days hit, you will be ready. Nothing is more frustrating than having a great idea and not having the supplies you need! If you have an accurate list to work from, you will not have to go from memory. The last thing anyone needs these days is one more thing to remember. Furthermore, a photocopy of the list will fit into your purse or pocket easier than the whole book.

I have marked the most essential supplies with a ★ . If you begin by collecting the supplies marked with a ★ you will have the supplies that are the most versatile and can be use in a number of different activities. Then, as you and your children work through your supplies and the activities, you can add to your growing stockpile and before long you will have many or most of the supplies needed to set up any of the activities in the entire book.

Grocery Store

Alphabet Pasta Letters (Collage, Soup)
Aluminum Foil (Props)★
Balloons (Volleyball)★
Bean Soup Mixes (Sorting)
Borax (Silly Putty)
Bubbles (Miscellaneous Fun)★
Cheerios (Stringing)★
Cheese Grater (Shred Crayons)
Clothespins (Sponge Painting)
Coffee Filters (Tie-dye)★
Colored Paperclips (Sorting)
Cookie Cutters (Lot of Things)★
Cornmeal (Cornmeal Sandbox)★
Cornstarch (Goop)★
Cotton Balls (Collage)
Deck of Cards (Memory)
Dried Beans, (Sorting, Collage)
   Pinto,Kidney,Black Eyed Peas
Elmers glue (Collage, Silly Putty)★
Flour (5 lbs) (Playdough)★
Food Coloring (Lots of Things)★
Fruit Loops (Stringing, Collage)
Gelatin (Jello Jigglers)
In the Shell Peanuts (Peanut Butter)
Ivory Snow (Bathtub Crayons)
Jello Mold (Ice Painting)
Jello Mix (Any Flavor) (Jigglers)
Karo Syrup (& Food Coloring)
Kiks Cereal (Stringing)
Kitchen Gadgets (Indoor Sandbox)★
   (Measuring Cups & Spoons,
Funnels, Plastic Utensils)
Kool-Aid (Unsweetened) (Playdough)★
Liquid Artificial Flavoring (Pancakes)
Macaroni (Stringing)★
Muffin Tins (Sorting)
Pancake Mold (Pancakes)★
Paper Plates (Miscellaneous Fun)★
Paper Muffin Cups (Sorting)
Pre-made Biscuits (Alphabet Food)
Pre-made Cookie Dough (Alphabet
Food)
Pizza Cutter (Playdough)
Popcorn (Popcorn Soup)
Popsicle Molds (Popsicles)
Popsicle Sticks (Popsicles)
Pudding (Finger painting with)★
Q-tips (Painting)★
Rice (10-20lbs) (Rainbow Rice)
Rubbing Alcohol (Lots of Things)★
Salt (Playdough)
Salt Shakers (Sprinkle Painting)
Shaving Cream (Finger painting with)
Sponges (Sponge Painting)
Wire Mess Strainer (Indoor Sandbox)
Straws (Lots of Things)★
Suction Cup Soap Holders (Mixing
Colors)
Timer (To smooth clean up time)
Toothpicks (Food Fun)
Unsweetened Soft Drink Mix
(Dinosaur Eggs)
Vano° Liquid Starch (Sidewalk Chalk)
Vegetable Oil (Playdough)
Vinegar (Dyed Eggs)
Wax Paper (Stained Glass)
Weird Vegetables (Food Fun)
Whipped Cream (Finger painting)
Yarn or String (Stringing)
Zip Lock Bags (Misc. Storage)

Hardware Store

Clothespins (Sponge Painting)
Elmers glue (Lots of Things)★
Flashlight (Flashlight Tag)
Magnets (Magnet Box)
Magnifying Glass (Misc. Fun)
Marbles (PVC & Marbles)
Masking And/or Duct Tape (Misc.)
Mirror (Dancing)
Nails (Woodworking)
PVC Pipe and Connectors
Scraps of Wood (Woodworking)
Small Hammers & Nails
(Woodworking)
Shallow Tub (Indoor Sandbox)★
Suction Cup Soap Holders (Mixing
Colors)
Very Fine Grit Sandpaper (Melted
Crayon Art)
Wallpaper Scraps (Misc. Fun)
Wooden Dowels (Fishing Poles)

Craft Store
Big Black Felt Pen (Silhouettes)
Bubbles (Misc. Fun)★
Confetti (Collage, Balloon Volleyball)
Construction Paper (Lots of Things)★
Crayons (Lots of things)★
Elmers glue (Lots of Things)★
Feathers (Collage)
Beads (Sorting)★
Bean Bags (Basketball)
Butcher Paper (Silhouettes)★
Buttons (Sorting)
Children's Scissors (Misc. Fun)★
Colored Cellophane (Flashlight Tag)
Colored Golf Tees (Sorting)
Drawing Paper (Misc. Fun)★
Eye Droppers (Mixing Colors)
Fake Fish (Fishing Game)★
Fingerpaint Paper (Finger painting)
Glitter (Misc. Fun)
Large Sheets of Paper (Painting Etc.)
Magnets (Magnet Box)
Magnifying Glass (Misc. Fun)
Marbles (PVC Pipe & Marbles)★
Ping Pong Balls (Straws and Ping
Pong Balls)
Play Money (Dress up Play)★
Popsicle Sticks (Popsicles)
Regular Watercolor Paints (Painting)★
Rubber Cement (Resist Painting)
Scraps of Material (Collage)
Sequence (Collage)

Sidewalk Chalk (Misc. Fun)★
Stamp with Stamp Pads (Misc. Fun)★
Stencils (Misc. Fun)★
Stickers (Misc. Fun)★
Tapestry Needles (Stringing)★
Tempra Paint (Painting)
Tissue Paper (Colored)
Watercolor Paintbrushes (Toast Art)
Watercolor Felt Pens (Misc. Fun)★
Watercolor Paints (Misc. Fun)★
Wooden Dowels (Fishing Poles)
Yarn or String (Lots of Things)★

Misc. Items
Adding Machine Tape (Table Top
Activities)
Colored Golf Tees (Sorting)
Cow Magnets (Magnet Box)
Deck of Cards (Memory Game)
Golf tees (Woodworking)
Exercise Trampoline (Misc. Fun)★
Exercise Video for Children (Misc.
Fun)★
Glycerine (To Make Bubbles)
Kitchen gadgets: (Indoor Sandbox)★
 Measuring cups
 Spoons
 Funnels
 Egg Beaters
 Garlic presses
 Spatulas etc.
Bowls & Lids

Sifters
Nerf Ball (Basketball)
Ping Pong Balls (& Straws)
Plastic Golf Balls (With PVC)
Poker Chips (Sorting)
Scarves (Dress up)
Scraps of Material (Misc. Fun)★
Sturdy Fabric (Building a Town)
Wallpaper Scraps (Collage)

Thrift Shop Items
Books
Cheese Grater
Dress up Clothes
Jello Molds
Iron
Kitchen Gadgets
Magnifying Glass
Muffin Tins
Real Phones★
Rollerskates
Puzzles
Shower Curtain
Toys

Order Form

■ **Online Orders: Please visit Amazon.com**

■ **Postal Orders: At-Play Publishing, P.O. Box 23012, San Jose, Ca 95123, USA.**

⇨ **Each book costs $12.95 plus tax, shipping and handling.**

Please send me _____ copies of *Mommy's Rainy Day Survival Guide*. *Please print clearly*.

Name: _____

Address: _____

City: _____ State: _____ Zip: _____

Sales Tax: Please add 8.00% ($1.04) for books shipped to California addresses.
Shipping: Book Rate: $2.75 for the first book and .75¢ for each additional book (Surface shipping may take three to four weeks) Priority Mail: Please add $3.50 per book.

Contact Information: Linda McKnight is available for parenting and teacher workshops. Lectures include fun and entertaining "hands-on" demonstrations of activities in the book as well as informative discussion about brain growth and development in young children. For further information please contact:

At-Play Publishing
P.O. Box 23012
San Jose, Ca. 95123
(408) 227-9505

Order Form

■ **Online Orders: Please visit Amazon.com**

■ **Postal Orders: At-Play Publishing, P.O. Box 23012, San Jose, Ca 95123, USA.**

⇨ **Each book costs $12.95 plus tax, shipping and handling.**

Please send me _____copies of *Mommy's Rainy Day Survival Guide*. ***Please print clearly***.

Name: _____

Address: _____

City: _____ State: _____ Zip:_____

Sales Tax: Please add 8.00% ($1.04) for books shipped to California addresses.
Shipping: Book Rate: $2.75 for the first book and .75¢ for each additional book (Surface shipping may take three to four weeks) Priority Mail: Please add $3.50 per book.

Contact Information: Linda McKnight is available for parenting and teacher workshops. Lectures include fun and entertaining "hands-on" demonstrations of activities in the book as well as informative discussion about brain growth and development in young children. For further information please contact:

At-Play Publishing
P.O. Box 23012
San Jose, Ca. 95123
(408) 227-9505